COLLINS GEM

PUB GAMES

The Diagram Group

HarperCollins*Publishers*

HarperCollins Publishers
P. O. Box, Glasgow G4 0NB

A Diagram Book first created by Diagram Visual
Information Limited of 195 Kentish Town Road, London
NW5 8SY

First published 1993

Reprint 10 9 8 7 6 5 4 3 2 1 0

© Diagram Visual Information Limited 1993

ISBN 0 00 470141 0
Printed in China

Introduction

How is marrow dangling like Old English skittles? Is toad-in-the-hole an animal racing game? Is nine men's morris a kind of dance? All is revealed in the *Collins Gem Pub Games* which brings together in one volume these and nearly 100 more of the best-loved and new-fangled public house pastimes. Included are aiming games like marbles and quoits, tabletop games like snooker and dominoes, board games like backgammon and draughts, and card and dice games like bridge and crown and anchor. In addition to long-time pub game favourites like skittles, shove ha'penny and nine men's morris, the book describes the pure lunacy of dwyle flunking, whose origins are unknown, as well as the very recent pinball and karaoke. Several record games – in which players compete to beat a record time or distance – are included, from the Australian import of wellie wanging to the traditional British yards of ale. Each game is described in detail, and its history, rules and practice are clearly explained using step-by-step instructions and clear illustrations. As a handbook, the guide will allow even the novice to join in any game. As a reference book, it will amuse and surprise. Created by the Diagram Group, the *Collins Gem Pub Games* is an attractive companion volume to the same team's *Gem Card Games, Gem Travel Games* and *Card Games 2*.

4

Contents

3. BOARD GAMES

4. CARD AND DICE GAMES

5. MISCELLANEOUS GAMES

5. MISCELLANEOUS GAMES (cont.)

About pub games

So-called typical pubs may be on their way to
becoming a rarity, but they can be found – and even in
the newer, brassier pubs taking hold a wealth of
pastimes are played, both modern and traditional. The
games described in this book cover a range from
ancient ones like nine men's morris to the fairly recent
wellie wanging; from those requiring great skill like
darts to those needing only bluff and bluster, like spoof.
Some were invented as pub games. Others, including
card games and dominoes, originated abroad and were
transported to Britain to be enjoyed in both public
houses and private parlours. Most can be learned: the
basic rules and some regional variations are described
here to get the novice started.

History

Pub games have a history of disapproval on the part of
the authorities – and not always with the intention of

restricting gambling. The earliest known restriction on
pub games was probably a statute during Henry VIII's
reign which was intended to keep men from being
distracted away from their archery duties. The
particular game they were targetting may have been
shove ha'penny, which was immensely popular among
the Tudors. The game is still one of the most frequently
played in pubs – evidence of the durability of many pub
games.

Gambling

Traditionally cards were played as gambling games in
pubs, and the authorities declared them unsuitable for
the lower classes, for whom gambling was thought to
be dangerous. For centuries, therefore, card games were
illegal in public houses but quite widely played at court
and in the parlours of the rich.

To this day, cribbage is the only card game that can be
played legally for small stakes throughout Britain. It is
left up to regional magistrates, however, to allow other
games to be played, resulting in the odd situation that
makes bridge, for instance, an approved gambling game
in one region but outlawed in the next. Gambling is not
permitted in pubs in Scotland.

All the games included in this book can be played and
enjoyed as non-gambling games.

Types of activities
Pub names often originate from the games played in
them, many relating to sports involving animals – The
Fighting Cocks, The Dog and Ducks. 'Ratting' was a
popular pub game in the 18th and 19th centuries:
players bet on which dog could kill the most rats
running loose in the pub. Fortunately, such illegal and
cruel sports are rarely found in today's pubs. It is
possible, however, to find examples of games involving
racing animals, including ferrets, insects, even maggots.

In addition to traditional, and even ancient, pastimes, many completely new games have appeared in pubs in recent years. With few exceptions, they differ from the traditional games in two significant respects: they are based on new technology and cost money to play. In many of these games, such as pinball and slot machines, the player's opponent is a machine rather than another player.

Enjoyment

The pub has long been the neighbourhood entertainment spot. Although the profit pubs make is in the sale of alcohol, it is not unreasonable to go to pubs for social encounters and not drink at all. Games, like drink, are an important component of pub life, as important as the beer for attracting both newcomers and regulars to many pubs. Some games even involve drinking to some extent, though most described in this book are for drinkers and non-drinkers alike.

In spite of the variety of games included in this book, they have several things in common. Most pub games are easily learned and so can be enjoyed by beginners as well as experienced players. Also, they tend to be playable by any number of people, allowing for the mixed sizes of groups that gather in such places. In addition, although many are a test of skill and are intended to be played competitively, all are meant, ultimately, to be enjoyed.

1. Aiming games

Some of the oldest and most traditional pub games are those involving aiming skills. Here are described several favourites, ranging from the quite simple – such as conkers – to the more complicated quoits.

Indoor games

CONKERS

Children and adults have played conkers for generations wherever horsechestnut trees, source of the conkers, are a feature of the landscape. Over the years, several English pubs have made a name for themselves by organising conker contests for their customers. The Chequered Skipper, an old pub at Ashton, near Oundle in Northamptonshire, claims to have the oldest conker club, formed in 1865. They host the World Conker Championships, held annually on the second Sunday in October. The Green Man in Little Braxstead, Essex, holds a conker contest every November; The Brown Cow at Norden, near Rochdale, Lancashire, holds theirs on Boxing Day.

The conkers

The game is usually played with nuts from the horsechestnut tree, but is sometimes played with hazelnuts (often called 'cobnuts'). To prepare their conkers, players make a hole through the centre

with a sharp instrument such as a meat skewer or a
compass point. Many players then harden their conkers
by soaking them in vinegar or salt and water and/or
baking them for about half an hour. For excellent
results, players may store their conkers in the dark for a
year.

When the conker is ready, a strong piece of string or a
bootlace, about 35–40cm (13–15in) is threaded through
the hole and knotted at one end. The string should be
long enough for about 25cm (9in) to hang down after it
is wrapped once or twice around the hand.

The game

Conkers is for two players. The player whose conker is
to be hit first holds the conker as shown (**a**) – with the
string wrapped round the hand. The height of the hand
is adjusted to suit the striker, and the conker must be
kept perfectly still for the hit.

The striker takes his or her conker in one hand and
holds the opposite end of the string in the other hand
(**b**). For the strike, the player draws the conker back and
then releases it in a fast swinging motion in the
direction of the opponent's conker (**c**).

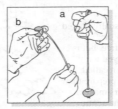

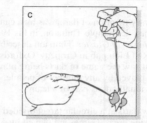

A striker who misses the opponent's conker is allowed a maximum of two further attempts to make a hit. After a hit is made, that player's turn ends and the opponent becomes the striker.

If the players' strings tangle, the first player to call 'strings' can claim an extra shot.

Ending the game

Play continues with players taking alternate turns until one of the conkers is destroyed – i.e. until no part of it remains on the string. The player who destroyed the conker wins.

Scoring

Conkers are usually described according to the number of victories won with them – e.g. a 'one', a 'fiver', a 'seventy-fiver'.

A conker increases its title by one each time it destroys a conker that has never won a game. A conker that defeats a conker with previous wins claims one for defeating it plus all the defeated conker's wins – so a 'fiver' that defeats another 'fiver' becomes an 'elevener'.

DARTS

The first literary mention of darts was by a canal
traveller named E. Temple Thurston, in his 1911 book
called *The Flower of Gloster*. Thurston describes his
visit to The Red Lion pub in Cropedy, Oxfordshire,
where he first saw the game of darts being played.
Darts can be played by any number of people, each
playing individually or as part of a team.

Aim

Players throw darts at a circular target divided into
different scoring areas. Games are played by
individuals, pairs or teams. In the standard game,
players aim to reduce a starting score exactly to zero.
Other games provide a great variety of objectives
designed to test the players' skill.

Darts

Each player has a set of three darts. Designs vary, but
most darts are about 15cm (6in) long. All darts have a
sharp point, usually made of steel; a barrel, made of
metal (usually brass), plastic weighted with metal or
wood; and a tail 'flighted' with feathers, plastic or
paper.

Good darts are essential: the most significant
development in the game may have come around 1930
in Britain, with the production of precision-made metal
darts by Frank Lowy, a Hungarian immigrant. He called
them Silver Comets and sold them in sets of three.
Another type of weighted darts was made in France and
known as French Darts.

The 1970s saw the introduction of extremely slim
titanium/tungsten darts, but many people still prefer the
fatter, brass-barrelled variety.

Dartboards

Most dartboards are made of cork, bristle or elm, with
the divisions and sector numbers marked by wires. The
standard tournament board is 45.5cm (18in) in diameter
and has 20 sectors, an outer 'doubles' ring, an inner
'trebles' ring, and an inner and outer 'bull' in the
centre. Adjacent sectors are differentiated by colour.
The evolution of dartboards has produced a variety of
designs. The London trebles board is the one most
commonly used throughout the world, mainly due to
standardisation for world championships.

The London
board

There are dozens of others still to be found in use in
local leagues. The old wide and narrow East London
Fives boards are still used in Poplar, Canning Town,
Bow and places outside London in Kent and Sussex.
In the Belgian–French border villages, the original
game of Vogelpic is still played on an 18cm (7in)
diameter board divided into six scoring segments, while
Vogelpic-Engelse is also played on the standard
London board.

**The Manchester
board**

The 25cm (10in) diameter Manchester or Lancashire
board, used by some darts leagues in the northwest of
England, has no trebles, a unique numbering
arrangement and an extremely narrow doubles ring.
The Old House at Home is the quaint name of a pub in
Withington, Manchester, where the Manchester board is
used. In the Hull area on the east coast of Britain, the
local brewery and newspaper run a league contest using
the Yorkshire board, which has no trebles but is
numbered the same as the London board.

**The Yorkshire
board**

In a pub called The Struggler, near Lincoln Cathedral, both the local Lincoln board and a standard London board are available, as they are in probably 40 other pubs in the area. The Lincoln board is similar to the Yorkshire board and is used for local league games. During the 1980s a new board was produced in Britain, known as The Champion's Choice. It is a standard London board with narrower doubles and trebles designed to improve a player's aim in practice.

In 1991 a British company produced yet another variation on the London board called the Quadro 24D which has a quadruple ring between the doubles and trebles rings. Its maximum score is 240, made by getting all three darts in quadruple 20.

Playing area

The dartboard is hung on a wall, with the centre 1.74m (5ft 8in) from the ground. Toe lines may be marked on a mat or on the floor, at 2.4m (8ft), 2.6m (8ft 6in) and 2.7m (9ft) from the dartboard. The scoreboard is a slate or blackboard, usually positioned to one side of the dartboard. Each side's score is recorded in chalk.

Starting

Each player, or one member of each pair or team, must get a dart in the doubles ring to begin scoring. The starting double is scored, as are darts thrown after but not before it in the same turn.

Turns

In singles games, opponents take turns to throw three darts each. In pairs and team games, one player from each side throws three darts in turn, with members of each side playing in the order established at the start of the game.

The first turn goes to the player, pair or team that wins the toss of a coin or gets a dart nearest the bull in a preliminary throw.

Playing area

Scored throws

A throw is invalid if the player is not behind the toe line when throwing.

Only those darts sticking in the board at the end of a

player's turn are scored. Thus darts are not scored if
they rebound, stick in another dart, fall from the board
or are knocked out before the player ends the turn.
Re-throws are not permitted. (Also note starting and
finishing procedures.)

Scoring
Scored throws are deducted from a starting total –
usually 301, 501 or 1001.

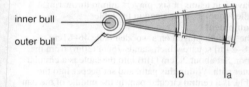

inner bull

outer bull

b   a

Darts in the inner bull score 50, and in the outer bull 25.
Darts in a sector score according to the sector number –
unless they are within the outer (doubles) ring (**a**),
when they score double the sector number, or the inner
(trebles) ring (**b**), when they score three times the sector
number.

Finishing
The game ends with a double bringing the score exactly
to 0. If the total in a turn takes the score past 0, or to 1,
the player goes back to the score before that turn and
forfeits any darts remaining in that turn.

EVESHAM QUOITS

Sometimes known as dobbers but more often as table
quoits, this is a genuine indoor version of outdoor
quoits. It is found in pubs in the English counties of
Gloucester, Hereford, Worcester and the Welsh
Borders, especially Powys. The rules of the Evesham
and District Quoits League, which flourished in the late
1970s, are generally used.

Aim

Playing in teams of six, players aim to throw rings,
called 'quoits', over a peg in the table.

Equipment

The game is played on a wooden table 46–61cm
(18–24in) square which stands 76cm (30in) from the
floor. Set about 2.5cm (1in) into the table is a circular
outer path. Within this path, and set deeper into the
table, is a central circular pan. In the middle of the pan
is a peg about 15cm (6in) high.

Each player has four rubber quoit rings. These vary in
diameter, thickness and weight. Usually they are
painted white on one side and are black on the other.
Behind the table there is usually a net to catch quoits
that overshoot.

Playing

The throwing distance varies by area: in Powys, for
example, players stand 24m 15cm (8ft 6in) from the
board; in the Evesham area, the distance is 27m 8cm
(9ft 3in); and it is up to 33m (11ft) in some pubs.

The most points can be scored by throwing the quoit
over the peg, white side up. This is known as 'spiking'.
A quoit that lands white side up in either the inner pan
or outer path scores as well, but both are worth fewer

points than a spike. Quoits landing black side up are considered dead and do not score, even if they ring the peg.

In league games there are six players to a team, and a match consists of six singles games and three pairs games.

The Evesham quoits table

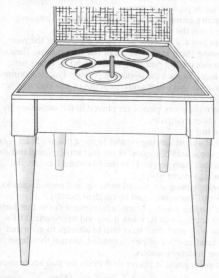

In singles games, teams toss a coin, or a quoit, for first throw. A member of the team winning the toss begins by throwing his or her four quoits. Then a member of the opposing team throws four quoits. The two players continue to throw alternately until one of them has made a score of exactly 61 points to win the first singles game.

Five more singles games are played in the same way by the other players in turn.

In pairs games, team members pair up to challenge a pair from the opposing team.

Pairs toss for first throw. The first player of the pair winning the toss throws his or her four quoits. Then one of the opposing pair throws, followed by his or her partner and then the opposing partner. Players continue to play in this order until the score of one pair reaches exactly 121.

Two more pairs games are played in the same way by the other four pairs.

Scoring

The standard scoring system in most pubs is 5:2:1 – i.e. a spike scores 5, a quoit in the pan scores 2 and one on the outer path scores 1. In the Evesham League, the scoring system is 4:3:1.

Singles games are played to 61 up and pairs games to 121 up. The score must be reached exactly.

In a singles game, players who make a throw that busts their score – that is, takes it beyond the required 61 – must wait until their next turn to attempt to get exactly the final number of points needed, even if they have some unthrown quoits.

In a pairs game, a player who busts the pair score over

121 will hope that his or her partner will get the correct number of points needed, unless the opposing players win in their turn.

VARIATION: SPIKES UP

This variation is played for money by experienced enthusiasts. The game is played between two individuals who agree a stake before they begin.

The first player tries to get as many consecutive spikes as possible. If spikes are made with all four of a player's quoits, the quoits are retrieved and thrown again, and so on.

If the player fails to get a spike, any remaining quoits are thrown and the player then adds any odd points gained to his or her total.

The opponent then throws in the same manner. The opposing player's aim is to exceed the first player's total and win the stake.

New stakes are then bet and another game begins. If the second player makes exactly the same score as the challenger, then the first player gets a chance to win by exceeding that score.

Sometimes the standard Evesham indoor quoits game is called round-the-board because the scoring is done on a standard cribbage board.

OLD ENGLISH SKITTLES

This is a strenuous game of skittles that has been played in London pubs for about 450 years. The game may still be observed at pubs in Ealing and Putney. At the time of writing there was still an Old English skittle alley in the basement of The Freemasons Arms, where the Hampstead Lawn Billiards, Quoits and Skittle Club has existed since 1888.

The alley

The length of the alley, or run, can vary; originally it was about 11m (36ft) long, and at The Freemasons Arms it is 6.4m (21ft) long. It is set 10cm (4in) into the floor.

An Old English skittles alley

At the beginning of the run is a storage rack for the 'cheeses' which the player throws in order to knock down the nine substantial pins that stand on a diamond-shaped platform at the other end of the run.

The platform is 1.8m (6ft) square and surrounded by a frame of hornbeam which stands just higher than the run. Set in the platform are nine brass plates on which the pins stand. A canvas backing catches any stray cheeses.

The pins

Made from hornbeam, each of the nine pins weighs 4kg (9lb). They stand 37cm (14.5in) high and in diameter are 8cm (3in) across the top and 17cm (6.5in) across the central belly. Replacing pins that are knocked down is a tough exercise in itself.

The cheeses

Made of lignum vitae, the cheese is disc-shaped and varies from 22 to 30cm (8.5 to 12in) across. Each cheese weighs between 1.8 and 2.7kg (4 and 6lb). It takes strength and excellent coordination to throw a cheese accurately.

Players

Individuals or pairs play against each other in casual games, but for matches there are two teams of six players each.

Playing

After tossing a coin for first throw, each player can throw up to four cheeses at each turn. A turn is known as a 'frame' or 'chalk'.

The aim is to knock down the pins with as few throws as possible. Scores are calculated as the number of throws it takes to knock down all the pins.

The player must hold the cheese in only one hand and is allowed only one short stride before throwing.

Scoring

Points are scored by the number of cheeses thrown to knock down all nine pins.

If a player knocks nine pins down with one throw, the throw is called a 'floorer', and the player scores 1 point. If the opponent's score is higher, the first player wins the chalk. If the opponent also makes a floorer, both players win half a chalk.

If a player knocks down eight pins with the first cheese, it is assumed the remaining pin would be knocked down with the next cheese, so the player scores 2 points without having to make the second throw. The same principle applies whenever one pin remains: the player scores one more point than the number of throws made so far without having to make the next throw.

Similarly, if a player has thrown all four cheeses in a turn and some pins still remain standing, a score of 5 points is given, on the assumption that the player would have managed to clear the frame had a fifth cheese been thrown.

The maximum and minimum points that can be scored by each player in a chalk are 5 and 1. The winner of a chalk is the player with the lower score.

The bolter

When the cheese goes through the pins without knocking down any of them, the shot is called a 'bolter'. It automatically loses the chalk, unless both players throw a bolter, in which case neither get the chalk. Bolters are greeted with sympathetic noises and cries of disbelief!

Winning

The game goes to the player who first wins seven chalks. In some competitions, the game is played to eleven chalks.

Techniques

The flooring shot is the ultimate aim of all players. The right-handed player can make a flooring throw as shown in the diagram.

How a floorer knocks down all nine pins

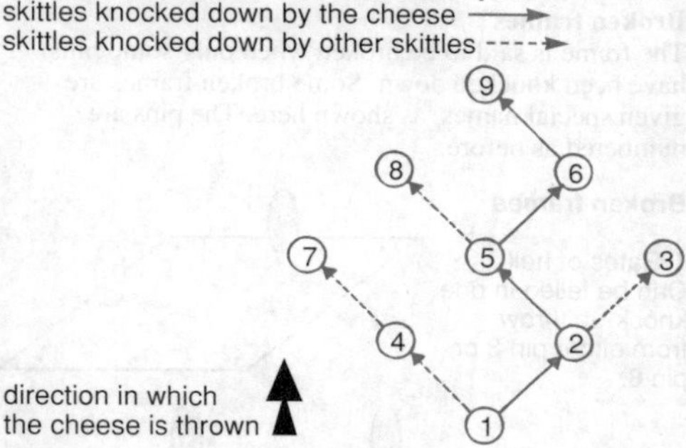

skittles knocked down by the cheese ⟶

skittles knocked down by other skittles ⤏

direction in which the cheese is thrown ▲

The action of the cheese thrown right-handed

At pin 1 The cheese hits the leading pin on its left shoulder at just the correct angle, knocking it over towards pin 4, which in turn falls over, knocking down pin 7.

At pin 2 The cheese rebounds to hit pin 2, which falls down hitting pin 3, which also falls down.

At pin 5 The cheese then rebounds off pin 2, knocking over pin 5, which knocks down pin 8.

At pin 6 The cheese finally hits pin 6 and rebounds to knock down pin 9. In the perfect floorer, the cheese would come to rest just over the back corner of the frame.

Playing left-handed

Left-handed players should aim for the leading pin's right shoulder; the pins will be hit by the cheese in order: 1, 4, 5, 8, 9.

Broken frames

The frame is said to be broken when only some pins have been knocked down. Some broken frames are given special names, as shown here. The pins are numbered as before.

Broken frames

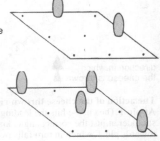

1 Gates of hell
Can be felled in one knock-on throw
from either pin 8 or
pin 6.

2 London Bridge
with police officer
This broken frame
is impossible to
clear in one throw.

RINGBOARD/HOOPLA

In 19th-century England, especially in northwest towns such as Bolton, Warrington and Oldham, ringboard was a very popular pub game, but it was generally overtaken by darts between the two world wars.

Keen teams of ring players still play league matches in Dagenham, Essex, and on Tuesdays during the winter months in pubs at Ventnor on the Isle of Wight. The Ventnor game uses a 15-hook board and throws over a distance of 2m (8ft) to score 201 points.

Equipment

The board Boards of different shapes and sizes are generally easy to buy – or may be made by the do-it-yourself enthusiast from plywood, hardboard or chipboard. Most bought boards are diamond- or shield-shaped, about 46cm (18in) high, and decorated with brightly coloured patterns or illustrations.

Screwed into the boards are a number of hooks – usually between twelve and sixteen. A figure below each hook indicates the number of points scored whenever a player throws a ring into the hook. The back of a ringboard has a thin rope loop for hanging the board on a wall or door.

Rings At least six rings should be provided. Bought rings are usually made of rubber and are about 8cm (3in) in diameter. They are similar to those used on jars of homemade preserves – these could easily be substituted. Other ideas for improvised rings are large curtain rings, or rings made from string or heavy card.

Playing

Any number of players throw as individuals or as team members.

Taking turns, each player stands an agreed distance
from the ringboard and throws six rings.

Scoring

At the end of the turn, each player scores the designated
number of points for each ring on a hook.

The game is won by the player or team with the most
points after an agreed number of throws.

Scoring variations

In the Lancashire version of rings, the aim was to move
round the board twice in numerical order, 1 to 13. Two
rings on the same number, known as doubles, also
counted – e.g. after a double 6, the player aimed for 13.
There is a genuine, circular rings board on display at
The Rose and Crown in Kirkhampton, Cumbria. It has
hooks numbered 1 to 13, the aim being to make a score
of 31. At an inn near Winchester in Sussex, the aim was
to make a score of 121.

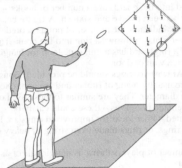

RINGING THE BULL

This game is believed by some to have been first played by the Romans, but a pub in Nottingham claims it was brought from Jerusalem during the Crusades. The pub is still called The Trip to Jerusalem, because crusaders stayed there on journeys to and from the Holy Land. Many pubs claim their game of ringing the bull to be unique, and indeed there are many variations.

VARIATION: PIG'S SNOUT

This is a modern variation of ringing the bull, launched during the 1980s by the Little Pub Company. It is now played in many British pubs, including The Sow and Pigs at Toddington, Bedfordshire.

Equipment

A life-size model of a pig's head is made of fibreglass and mounted on a green baize board, hung on the wall.

A string hangs from the ceiling in front of the head. On its end is a solid rubber object similar in shape to those used to protect the base of walking sticks.

Playing

Small coins are balanced on the pig's snout and ears. Taking turns, each player swings the rubber and tries to knock off the coins, gaining 2 points for the nose coin and 1 for an ear coin. The winner is the one who first reaches 11 points.

RINGOLETTE

Ringolette is another target game played with rings.

Equipment

Victorian ringolette sets usually contained ten or twelve small skittles and a similar number of wooden rings. A figure on each skittle indicated its points value.

The game can easily be played with improvised materials – such as rubber rings like the ones used for ringboard, and bottles instead of skittles. Make sure the ring fits around the entire bottle with some room to spare.

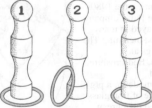

Playing

The game is for two players or teams.

In turn, each player stands an agreed distance from the targets and throws all the rings, attempting to get each one over a different target.

For a target with one ring over it at the end of the turn, a player scores the target's points value.

If any target has more than one ring over it, the player's opponent is awarded the points value of that skittle for each extra ring.

The game is won by the player or team scoring the most points.

TIDDLYWINKS

In old English dialect the word 'tiddlywink' was the name not only of a game but also of a beerhouse that had not been licensed as required under the 1869 Beerhouse Act. It is likely, however, that the game was already being played in the beerhouses, under a different name, long before the act was passed. Variations of the rules and aims can be found in tiddlywink games based on sports such as tennis and golf. The standard game is usually played by two, three or four players.

Playing area

Games are played on the floor or on a table. Any shape of table may be used but a square or round one is best if there are more than two players. The table should be covered with a thick cloth or piece of felt.

Equipment

Winks and shooters must be slightly pliable and are usually made of bone or plastic. Winks are usually about 2cm (0.8in) and shooters about 2.54cm (1in) in diameter. Each player has four winks and one shooter; these should be of a different colour than other players' pieces.

Target cups are made of plastic, wood or glass and are usually 4cm (1.5in) across and 2.5–5cm (1–2in) high.

Aim

In the standard game of tiddlywinks, each player attempts to put small discs or 'winks' into a cup by shooting them with a larger disc called a 'shooter'.

Playing

The cup is placed in the centre of the playing area, and players place their winks in a line in front of them.

Order of play is often decided by a preliminary shot –
the first shot of the game going to the player who
shoots nearest the cup. Play then proceeds clockwise
around the players.

Each player shoots one wink in a turn plus one extra
shot each time a wink goes into the cup.

Shooting

A player shoots a wink by stroking and pressing the
edge of the shooter against the edge of the wink and so
making the wink jump into the air. A wink is shot from
where it lies after the player's previous turn.

Out of play

Any wink that is partly covered by another is out of
play. A player whose wink is covered by an opponent's
wink must either wait until the opponent moves the
wink or must attempt to remove the opponent's wink by
hitting it with one of his or her own winks.

Any wink that stops against the side of the cup is out of play until it is knocked level onto the table by another wink.

A wink that is shot off the table does not go out of play, but is instead replaced on the table at the point where it went off.

Winning the game

The game is won by the first player to get all his or her tiddlywinks in the target cup.

Scoring

Tiddlywinks may be scored in two ways:

1 players count the number of games they win; or

2 players score 1 point for each wink they have shot in the cup when each game ends.

Outdoor games

AUNT SALLY

Aunt Sally was probably adapted from a 14th-century
skittles game known as club kayles and was preserved
in fairgrounds.

In the 1970s this simple form of outdoor skittles was
played at about 60 Oxfordshire pubs. The Oxford and
District League, whose headquarters were at The Prince
of Wales on Cowley Road, Oxford, had a fixture list
from April to September. Several pubs had two teams
in the league.

The Aunt Sally Association in Oxford publishes its own
official rule card, obtainable from pubs where the game
is still played.

The pitch

Aunt Sally is played on a pitch about 9m (30ft) long
with a canvas erected at the end opposite to the thrower.
When throwing, the player must stand behind a slightly
raised wooden marker known as the 'hocking'.

Equipment

The iron Just in front of the canvas a hollow metal rod
is driven firmly into the ground. This is known as the
'iron' and stands 76cm (30in) high. At the top of the
iron is a swivelled shelf the shape of a swan's neck on
which the skittle stands.

The doll The oak or beech skittle, which the player
aims to knock off the iron, is 15cm (6in) high and 10cm
(3.75in) in diameter. It is painted white and has a short
neck and wide shoulders and is known as the 'doll'.

The sticks Each player has six oak or beechwood
sticks, which are thrown so as to knock the doll off the
iron. The sticks are 46cm (18in) long and 4cm (1.75in)
in diameter, and weigh about 227g (8oz). Expert
players often have their own set of sticks.

The Aunt Sally doll and iron

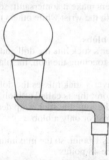

Players
The game is played between two teams of eight players.
In addition, there is one referee, an experienced player
known as the 'sticker-up'. The sticker-up keeps the
scores, decides if a hit has been made correctly and
replaces the doll after it has been hit.

Playing
The sticker-up tosses a coin to decide which team has
first throw.
Each member of the team that wins the toss throws his

or her six sticks in turn. Then the members of the
opposing team each play their six sticks, making a total
of 48 throws for each team.

Throwing techniques

The only rule about throwing is that sticks must always
be thrown underhand. Other than that, players tend to
develop their own styles. Some throw the stick end
first, and others make it somersault; some flick it
broadside with the wrist while others use a wide arm
throw.

Crosses and blobs

When a player's stick hits the doll and knocks it off the
iron, without touching the iron, the player scores a
'cross'.

When the player's stick misses the doll or hits the iron,
there is no score; this is called a 'blob'. If a stick hits
the doll and the iron, the sticker-up decides if it is an
acceptable cross or only a blob.

Scoring

A cross scores 1 point, so the maximum score for each
team would be 48 points.

After both teams have thrown, the team with the higher
score wins that round, known as the 'horse'. The team
that won the horse throws first for the next horse.

A match consists of three horses. The maximum match
score would be 144 points (3 x 48), if a cross were
scored on every throw in every horse – i.e. no player
made a blob. Although there is no record of anyone
making this maximum – 18 points in a match – the best
players can throw 5s or 6s fairly consistently. The
highest recorded team score was 40 crosses made in a
match at The Edward VII pub in Hinksey, Oxfordshire,

HORSESHOE PITCHING

An old game, horseshoes is played in Europe, South Africa and North America. Horseshoe pitching teams play regularly in Ireland and in Essex, England – in particular at The Horse and Groom at Wivenhoe, Colchester. The Queen's Head pub at Bulwick, Northamptonshire, has a fine horseshoe pitch where customers generally play to American rules. They hold an annual contest on New Year's Day.

The game is played on a pitching court with specially designed 'horseshoes', which are pitched at stakes from alternate ends of the court. The object is to pitch the horseshoe as close to the stake as possible.

A game may last for 50 pitches or until the first player or pair reaches 40 points, depending on the scoring system used.

The court

There are two pitching platforms separated by a pitching distance of 12.2m (40ft) [many courts allow a pitching distance of 9.15m (30ft) for women and players under 17]. Pitching platforms are flush with the ground on outside courts, but may be raised 15cm (6in) on indoor courts, which also require a minimum head-clearance of 3.65m (12ft).

The target areas are usually made of moist clay, sand or an artificial substance, so that the shoes do not bounce or roll when thrown.

The stakes are 58.5cm (23in) high and positioned in the centre of the target area.

The horseshoes

The shoes are produced specifically for pitching and must weigh a maximum of 1.19kg (2lb 1oz). They

have rolled-down edges called 'heel calks' and a 'toe
calk' on the closed end.

Contests

Two players usually play for the best of eleven games.
In tournaments, contestants play one game against each
of the other players. There may also be qualifying
rounds in order to divide the competitors into classes,
with the winners of each class then playing against each
other.

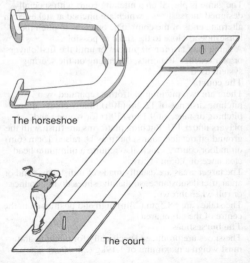

The horseshoe

The court

Singles matches involve two players with two shoes each. From the same platform, they take turns pitching two shoes each; all four shoes completes an inning. The players then walk to that stake, score the throws, and pitch back to the first stake.

Three players also can compete with each other in a three-handed game of singles.

Doubles matches require the partners in each pair to separate, so that one stands at either stake. The shoes are pitched from one platform first and are then pitched back by the other couple; no walking from stake to stake is involved.

The partners' scores are combined to give a final total, but a record of each of the players' pitches should be kept separately.

Playing

The player pitching must stand on one of the pitching platforms and in the specified area. He or she must stay behind the foul line until the shoe has been thrown.

The opposing player stands either in the rear of the other pitching platform or behind it, but the toes of one foot must be in contact with the platform.

No player can walk to the opposite stake until the inning has been completed.

Penalties

Opposing players must not talk, move, or in any way distract the pitcher. Otherwise their score for that inning is not recorded. Players also lose their inning score if they touch or move the pitched shoes before the scores have been awarded.

Scoring shoes

To qualify for the scoring, shoes must be within 15cm

(6in) of the stake. A shoe that first strikes the ground outside the target area is not counted in the score. A shoe thrown from an illegal position (outside the specified pitching area) is also disqualified. An opponent may ask for such shoes to be removed from the target area. A shoe that breaks on impact is not scored, but is removed and another pitch is taken.

A 'ringer' is a shoe that lands around the stake with enough space for a straight-edge to touch the shoe's prongs, but without touching the stake.

In three-handed games, if two players of one team score a ringer and the third does not, the third player's pitch is not scored.

Scoring methods

In **cancellation scoring**, a ringer scores 3 points. Each shoe that is closer than an opponent's pitch scores 1 point. The game continues until one player has reached 40 points.

Only the difference between the scores of the players is counted in each inning. Therefore, no score is recorded if equal points are scored in an inning. The scorer in one inning begins the pitching in the next, but if no points are scored the order alternates.

In **count-all scoring**, each ringer scores 3 points. A point is scored for every shoe pitched to within 15cm (6in) of the stake, regardless of the position of an opponent's shoes.

A game is made up of 25 innings, which means that a total of 50 shoes are pitched by each player, or by each pair in a doubles game.

The order of pitching alternates from one player or team to the other. A tie is decided by an extra inning.

KNUR AND SPELL

This outdoor bat-and-ball game is particularly popular in Lancashire and in Yorkshire, where the players are known as 'laikers'. Traditionally, each locality would have its own variation. There are a number of similar games called billets, nipsy, Peggy and poor man's golf.

Aim

The object is to hit the ball, called a 'knur', as far as possible by means of a sprung contrivance known as the 'spell'.

Equipment

The knur (also called the 'nurr', 'nur', 'nor', 'ner' and 'ore') is a round ball, about the size of a golf ball, made of wood, glass, lignum vitae, horn (weighted with lead) or ceramic. A pot knur was originally called a 'pottie'. The knur looks like a golf ball with a pitted or carved surface and weighs 14.17g (0.5oz).

It is usual to have several knurs available for a game; the weather and ground conditions determine which type is used. All players use the same knur throughout the match.

The bat (also called the 'pommell', 'kibble', 'tribet' and 'trevit') is specially made to get the right amount of spring when used. Traditionally, every laiker would own a set of bats, each with a head of different weight for changing conditions.

A bat consists of a shaft of ash or alder, anything from 61cm to 1.83m (2–6ft) long. At one end is a hand grip of rubber or cloth, and at the other the launching head. The head is round-backed with a flat striking surface 5–7.6cm (2–3in) wide. The head is made of boxwood, beech or sycamore.

A player about to strike

The spell is a 61cm (2ft) long piece of metal or wood fixed to the ground with a stake. On it is a sprung arm with a release catch and a screw with which to fix the tension of the spring.

In some versions, instead of a spell, the knur is launched from a sling hanging from a device known as the 'pin'.

How the player uses the spell

The knur sits on a little cup near the release catch. The player adjusts the tension screw according to how much spring is wanted in the arm. The player then stands back and taps the release catch with the bat. The knur is launched by the arm springing up as the catch is released.

The spell

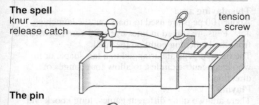

The pin

The pin is made of wood and has a strong upright about 1.22m (4ft) high and an L-shaped foot. Beneath the foot is a spike which holds the pin firmly when it is pushed into the ground. From the top of the pin an arm is held horizontally; from this arm is suspended a cord with a loop. This is the sling. The knur is placed in the loop and held steady by a wire running between the cord and the lower foot.

To launch the knur from the sling, the player hits it with the bat.

The playing area

About 100 pegs are used to mark out the launching
area. Pegs are staked in lines every 20 yards downwind
from the launching point on the spell.
The lines of pegs are arranged in a fan-shape, or in
whole concentric circles, to allow for changes of
direction.

Playing

There are two quite different games: long knock and
scores. The latter was the more serious, match game. In
the early 20th century, scores was played by
professionals with large financial stakes on their
performance.
Both games can be played by any number of players.

Long knock

Players play individually and their aim is to make the
longest hit, or 'knock', on a single strike, known as a
'rise'.
Each player has an agreed number of rises, usually 20,
played in batches of five.
In team matches, each player may have 15 rises, played
in batches of five.

Counting the distance

In either game, played from a spell or a pin, the
distance the knur is knocked is counted in scores, a
score being 20 yards, as marked by the pegs.
In long knock, the extra distance between two 20-yard
pegs is counted and added in feet. For example, a
player may make a knock of 6 score 21 feet (i.e. 120 +
7 = 127 yards), a relatively short knock.
The long knock record is said to be held by a Barnsley
man who, in 1899, knocked a pot knur 15 score 14 feet.

A man from Halifax, however, is claimed to have
bettered that knock in the same year with 18 score 12
yards 1.5 feet. Some people discount this claim because
his wooden knur bounced off a wall.

Scores

This is a much tougher game than long knock since
consistency is essential.

Each player has anything from 25 to 35 rises, played in
batches of five. The number of rises is agreed before
the match begins.

When counting the scores, only completed scores are
included, so each knock is a whole number of scores.
For example, the scores for a player's five rises might
be: 6; 9; 3; 10; 0 = 28. On the first rise, the player
knocked the knur beyond the 6-score line but not as far
as the 7-score line. In the next three rises, the knocks
were 9 scores, 3 scores and 10 scores consecutively. On
the last rise, the player missed hitting the release catch.
The winner of the scores match is the player with the
best overall score.

The 19th-century individual record, since bettered, was
367 scores in 30 rises. The record for a batch of five
rises was made at the turn of the century by a Yorkshire
player, whose score for his third batch of five rises was
14;15;15;13;13 = 70.

MARBLES

Games with marbles have been popular for thousands
of years and are played in countries all over the world.
Since 1926 The Greyhound Inn in Tinsley Green,
Sussex, has been the venue for the British Marbles
Championships held annually on Good Friday.
The marbles are small, hard balls made from stone,
wood, baked clay, plastic, glass or steel. They are
usually about 1.3cm (0.5in) in diameter. A marble used
by a player to shoot is often called a 'taw'.
The names and rules of marbles vary tremendously
from place to place, but the basic objective of any
marbles game is to test how accurately a player can aim
his or her marbles.

VARIATION: RING TAW

Ring taw, the ancient game of marbles preferred by adults, is particularly popular in the south of England. The game, for any small number of players, gets its name from the 1.8m (6ft) ring (usually of concrete) on which each player uses his or her personal tolley or taw marble – shooting marble – to knock up to 49 smaller marbles out of play.

The playing area

A circle about 2m (7ft) in diameter is drawn on the ground; inside this is drawn another circle, about 30cm (12in) in diameter.

Each player places one or two marbles into the innermost circle to begin the game.

Shooting

Marbles can be rolled along the ground or shot. Players can make the furthest and most accurate shots by 'knuckling down'. The knuckle of the forefinger is placed on the ground and the taw is balanced on the forefinger in front of the thumb, which is then released to shoot the marble.

Playing

In turn, each player shoots a marble from any point outside the larger circle, aiming toward the marbles in the inner circle.

The player keeps any marbles knocked out of the inner circle by the shot. In addition, the player wins an extra shot, which must be taken from where his or her taw landed.

If no marbles in the inner circle are hit, the turn ends. After each player has had a first turn, on subsequent turns players may aim to hit any marble in either circle,

including taws. Shots are always taken from where the
player's taw landed.

When a taw is hit, the taw's owner must pay the hitter
one marble.

Shooting or 'knuckling down'

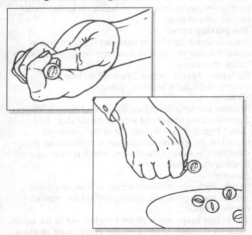

Winning the game

The game ends when all marbles have been shot out of
the innermost circle.

The player with the most marbles at the end of the
game wins.

MELL

Also known as pell mell, pall mall and lawn billiards, this game developed in Italy and the Netherlands in the 15th century. The aim of the game is to push balls through a ring using a cue. Hence some people think mell was a city-dwellers' version of croquet.

The game was popular for at least two centuries in the small city gardens and inn yards of London and its surrounding villages, such as Hampstead, Barnes and Notting Hill, which are now part of the metropolis.

Near St James Palace, King Charles II had an enormous pitch built which was 1000 yards long, called Pall Mall. The road of the same name has since been built on top of it.

The Freemason's Arms on Downshire Hill, Hampstead, in northwest London had the last standard mell pitch; it was abandoned in the 1980s, but there are plans to renew it.

The game is played on a small pitch at some inns in the low countries where it is called kolf.

The pitch

The standard pitch is a circle of wooden blocks, known as the carpet, 4.3m (14ft) in diameter, set in an outer circle of grass or shingle 7.3m (24ft) in diameter. The outer circle therefore forms a path round the carpet, 1.5m (5ft) wide. The path slopes downward towards a boundary retainer.

In the centre of the carpet an iron ring, 20cm (7.7in) in diameter, is fixed vertically. The ring rotates on its fixture.

Protruding from one side of the carpet is a flat, square apron which is opposite a starting platform, called the

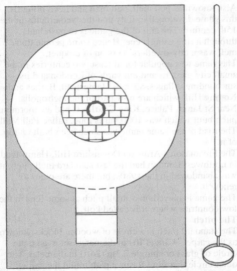

The mell pitch

The mell cue

'shoe', which sticks out from the whole pitch, making
the pitch keyhole-shaped. The shoe is 1.8m (6ft) wide.

Equipment

Four solid wooden balls are required, each weighing
3.6kg (8lb) and 19cm (7.5in) in diameter. Each player

has a shafted wooden pole 1.3–1.5m (4.5–5ft) in length, called a 'cue'. The cue has a metal ring at one end which is slightly smaller than 19cm (7.5in) in diameter. The cue ring is used to lift and push the balls.

Players

Singles is played between two people, each using two balls. Doubles is played between two pairs, each person using only one ball. Each player has a cue, all of which are the same length.

Playing

The rotating ring in the carpet is turned to face the shoe. Players toss a coin for order of play, then the first player places his or her ball on the wooden strip and holds a cue upright with both hands behind the ball, which the cue's ring just touches. The player attempts to push or toss the ball through the carpet ring.

All players make their first shot from the shoe. The first player has the advantage of facing the carpet ring when shooting, but subsequent players may find the angle of the ring has been altered by the first ball. Balls are played in strict order.

Scoring

A first throw that goes directly through the carpet ring scores 2 points. After each player's first shot, a ball that goes directly through the ring scores 1 point.

A ball that goes through the ring by bouncing off another ball is called a 'cannon' and can score 2 points if the two balls were at least one cue length apart before the shot was made.

In some games it is agreed that a player who knocks his or her ball off the carpet loses a point. That player's next turn must be shot from wherever the ball landed.

The game is won when a player or pair reaches a score of 21 points.

Techniques

The ball can be hit, pushed, lifted and tossed with the cue. With practice the ball can be given a top or a side spin. Cannon shots can be made from above as well as at ground level. Expert players learn to control the angle of the ring.

PÉTANQUE

The most popular bowling game in France, pétanque is spreading through Britain. The British Pétanque Association was formed at Sam's Hotel in Shedfield, Southampton, in 1974 after a customer returning from holiday in France started playing the game there a few years earlier.

Aim

Players try to throw steel balls, called 'boules', as close as possible to a smaller ball, known as the 'cochonnet' or 'jack'.

The pitch

There are precise international rules about size, but most social games are played on whatever land is available.

Any strip of unpaved ground about 11–12m (35–40ft) long will make a pitch. Sun-baked clay is the natural French surface. In Britain, a fine gravel pub yard is the most usual pitch.

Equipment

Modern boules are stainless steel, 7–8cm (2.7–3in) in diameter and weighing 620–750gm (22–26oz). The boules are often coloured.

The jack or cochonnet is a wooden ball 2.5–3cm (1–1.2in) in diameter. In Britain it is often painted white.

A tool called a 'baguette' – marked with measurements, like a ruler – is used to scratch a circle in the playing area and to measure small distances between boules and the cochonnet.

Players

The game can be played by singles, doubles (teams of two) or trebles (teams of three). The players use four, three or two boules each, respectively.

The most popular social game is doubles. League games are played in threes, but whatever the number the game is played in the same way.

The pitch

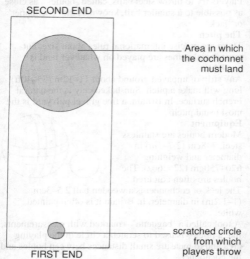

SECOND END

Area in which the cochonnet must land

scratched circle from which players throw

FIRST END

Preparing to play

A coin is tossed to decide who goes first.

The first player uses the baguette to scratch a circle round him- or herself 30–46cm (12–18in) in diameter at one end of the pitch. For the rest of the game, players must stand with both feet on the ground inside the circle when it is their turn to play.

The first player stands in the circle to throw the cochonnet. It must land in the area shaded on the diagram of the pitch shown here. If not, the player throws it again until it does.

Playing doubles

The person who threw the cochonnet throws the first boule, aiming to get it as close as possible to the cochonnet.

If a boule happens to land next to the cochonnet actually touching it, the throw is known as un tetard (tadpole) or un biberon (baby's bottle).

The opposing players then have to pitch their boules until one of them lands closer to the cochonnet than the first player's. All players may pitch all their boules. Only when the opposing team has a boule nearer the cochonnet than the first boule may the starting team play again.

Players play their own boules. When a team has used up its boules, the other team may continue to play until it too has no boules.

Scoring

Each boule that is closer to the cochonnet than its nearest rival gains 1 point. The baguette is used to measure small differences accurately.

Each round is known as an 'end'. The winner of the

first end starts the next round from the opposite end of the pitch at the position of the cochonnet. If the game runs to three ends, the third end is played from where the cochonnet was in the second end.

The circles in which players stand are rubbed out by foot as each end is completed.

The maximum score a doubles team can make in an end is 6 points. The game is played until one team reaches 13 points.

The team winning the last game plays first in the next game.

League play

Competitive matches are usually played between teams of three players, each with a particular skill:

1 the pointer, who is expert at getting the boule next to the cochonnet;

2 the shooter, who is expert at pushing the opposition boules out of the way and getting his or her own in their place;

3 the all-rounder, who is skilled at all the moves and takes charge of tactics. This player is usually the team captain.

QUOITS

Games in which iron rings are thrown have existed for centuries, and probably developed from horseshoe pitching. Quoits, one such ring game, grew in popularity, and by the early 19th century many travellers played with farmers and miners at their local inns.

Leagues were formed especially in northeast England, East Anglia, Scotland and Wales. In 1881 clubs from the northeast met at The Castle and Anchor, Stockton-on-Tees, and at The Princess Alice in Middlesborough, where they agreed a set of rules and formed the Association of Amateur Quoits Clubs of northern England. These Association rules are still used for quoits played at a few pubs in the northeast, such as The Wheatsheaf at Corbridge-on-Tyne just south of Hadrian's Wall in Northumberland.

The pitch

Quoits is played outdoors on a pitch, or a flat field, some 12.8–14.7m (14–15yd) long. At each end there is a flat clay bed 9.1m (3ft) square. At the centre of each bed is an iron peg standing about 5–8cm (2–3in) high, called the 'hob'.

The distance between the two hobs is 10m (11yd) and is known as the 'throwing distance'.

The clay bed

The quoits are sometimes thrown so that they stick into the clay bed; for this reason the clay is never allowed to dry hard. It is kept in good condition by placing wet sacks over it, with wooden planks on top, when not in use.

Deciding the winner using callipers

The quoits

Each player has two quoits. Made of iron, often by the local blacksmith, they are circular rings 12.7cm (5in) in diameter and weighing 22gm (5lb), although small variations exist to suit individual preferences.

Some old quoits had a chrome or silver finish and were lovingly polished by their owners.

The quoit is shaped like a saucer with a hole in the middle. The concave side is called the 'hole'; the convex side, the 'hill'.

Quoits resting on the hob

pot

black pot

Frenchman

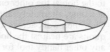

ringer

The aim

Players try to score a point by throwing their quoit closest to the hob. Getting the quoit hooked onto the hob, a very difficult task, scores 2 points.

A casual game

A game can be played between two or three individuals, each throwing a quoit in turn.

The player stands next to one of the hobs and throws towards the hob at the other end.

The quoit is held flat in the hand and the thumb and ends of the fingers are used to manipulate the angle of the quoit as it is thrown underhand.

After everyone has thrown a first quoit, a point is scored by the quoit nearest to the hob.

Players then throw their second quoit from the opposite end. The aim is to be the first to score either 11 or 15 points.

Playing a match

League matches are played between teams of eight people. Team members are paired with a member from the opposite team. Pairs toss a quoit for first throw, calling 'hill' or 'hole'.

The first pair of players stands next to a hob and throws to the hob at the other end. They throw their quoits one at a time, alternately, until all four have been thrown. They then walk across to the hob and measure which quoits are nearest the hob using a pair of callipers or any other handy tool for measuring. A scorekeeper notes their scores.

The same players throw again back to the first end as before. They continue to play until one player reaches 21 points. The clay beds may have to be flattened from time to time ready for the next throws.

The next pair throw, starting from the same end as the first pair, and score as before, playing to 21.

When all eight pairs have played, the team scores are totalled to determine which team has won the match. To speed up league matches, an inn might have two or more pitches side by side so that two or more pairs could play simultaneously.

A quoits glossary

A ringer is when a quoit lands over the hob. This scores 2 points. However, if the one player lands a ringer on top of another player's quoit, the player whose quoit is on top not only gains 2 points but also cancels the 2 points won by the first player.

A gater is when the quoit lands with its edge on the near side of the hob. If it is hill-side-up, it is called a 'hill-gater'; if hole-side-up, a 'hole-gater'.

A black pot is when the quoit lands with its edge on the far side of the hob.

A pot is when the edge of the quoit is on the left side of the hob. It is called a 'Frenchman' when the quoit's edge is on the right of the hob.

A bibber is a member of the thrower's own team who acts as a helper. The bibber stands near the hob at which the thrower is aiming and shouts advice, sometimes putting a scrap of paper on the spot where he or she thinks the thrower should aim. A bibber also risks getting hit by a bad throw!

The trig man (or woman) watches the thrower's feet and calls a foot fault if they are in front of the hob.

The marker keeps a tally of the scores.

The referee only gives decisions on disputes.

2. Table and tabletop games

The games in this chapter are all played on tables – both on specially constructed tables, as in pool and bagatelle, and on any smooth tabletop, as in dominoes and shovelboard.

BAGATELLE

Bagatelle became popular in Britain during the late 18th century. By the 1950s the game had nearly disappeared from London pubs, but it is still played in leagues in Chester and parts of north Wales, in Bristol, and in the midland cities of Walsall and Coventry.

The game described here is quite different from the children's game of bagatelle, described in the Board Games chapter (p.133).

Aim

The object is to land as many balls as possible into scoring cups on the table. Two players can compete with one another, or four can play in teams.

Equipment

Table The bagatelle table is 1.8–3m (6–10ft) long, 61–91cm (2–3ft) wide and 76cm (2.5ft) high. It has cushions like a billiard table, and one end is a semicircle.

At this end are nine shallow holes, or 'cups', each marked with a score from 1 to 9. They are arranged in a circle with 9 in the middle.

Balls and cue Each player has eight white, or 'cue', balls; one black ball is used by all players. Players shoot the balls with a wooden cue, as in billiards.

The bagatelle table

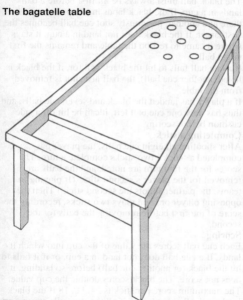

Playing

The first player or team places the black ball in front of the circle of cups – this is called 'spotting'. From the opposite end of the table, the player shoots all eight cue balls, one at a time, toward the black ball and the cups.

The black ball must always be hit first before a ball lands in a cup. If the black lands in a cup, it remains there and another, previously shot cue ball becomes the first target. If the black does not land in a cup, it stays where it came to rest on the table and remains the first target ball.

If a cue ball fails to hit the black ball (or, if the black is holed, another cue ball), the ball just shot is removed from the table.

If a player has landed the black and seven cue balls, and thus has only one cue ball left, it can be hit off a side cushion before scoring.

Completing a stick

After shooting all eight cue balls, the player has completed a 'stick'; two sticks complete a turn. The scores for the first turn are noted, and the balls are removed for the player's second stick. (If playing in teams, the partner shoots the second stick.) Then the opposing player or team plays two sticks, recording the score of the first before removing the balls for the second.

Scoring

Each cue ball scores the value of the cup into which it lands. If a cue ball does not land in a cup, or if it fails to hit the black (or another cue ball) before so landing, it does not score. The black scores double the cup value. The maximum score per stick is 54: i.e. 18 if the black lands in the 9 cup, plus 36 if all the cue balls are scoring.

Winning the game

The winner is the player or team with the highest score after an agreed number of turns.

BAR BILLIARDS

In spite of its name, bar billiards is more closely related to bagatelle than to any billiards game. Although waning in popularity, especially since the introduction of American pool, bar billiards is still played in Oxford, High Wycombe and on the Channel Islands; championships are held annually in Jersey and in Eastbourne, at the Lansdowne Hotel.

Equipment

Like pinball, bar billiards is played on a special coin-operated table, usually rented by the pub. Since its introduction in Britain in the 1930s, the price of a game has kept pace roughly with the average cost of a pint. The table, smaller than a standard billiards table, is

The bar billiards table

rectangular and has a raised backboard for scoring. Nine shallow holes at one end are marked with values for scoring, ranging from 10 to 200 points.

Two white pins are placed on both sides of the 100 hole, and one red pin is placed beside the 200 hole. Players compete against one another in a timed game; the internal clock usually allows between 15 and 20 minutes per game.

Playing

As in bagatelle, the aim is to shoot the cue ball so as to hit the red 'spot' ball and to 'hole' as many balls as possible. As balls are holed, they are returned to the player to be shot again.

The pins are obstacles rather than targets. If a white pin is knocked down, the player's turn ends and the opposing player takes a turn. If the red pin is knocked down, the player loses his or her entire score and begins again from 0.

Time up

Once the clock runs out the player shoots any balls remaining on the table. The final cue ball must rebound off a side cushion and land in the 200 hole; on this shot players must be careful not to knock down the red pin next to this hole and risk losing their entire score.

Winning the game

The player with the highest score at the end of the game wins. Very high scores can be achieved by expert players.

CAROM BILLIARDS

This is a popular game in the bars of India, Yemen, Burma and Switzerland, where it is called carombole. It has not had much success in English pubs, although The Sun, in Reading, Berkshire, once invited the current Swiss carombole champion to demonstrate the game. One or two pubs in Cheshire are said to have a carom table hidden away in the cellar.

Aim

The object of the game is to be the first player to reach an agreed number of points.

Equipment

The table The game is played on a billiards table without pockets. The table is 1.5m x 3m (5ft x 10ft); smaller tables can be found in some locations. Other features of the table, shown on the following page, include:

1 foot cushion	**6** head string
2 foot string	**7** head cushion
3 foot spot	**8** head spot
4 centre string	**9** diamond
5 centre spot	**10** side rails

The strings are only imaginary lines.

Cue and balls The game is played with three balls: one red and two white, one of which serves as the spot ball, or 'cue ball'. Each player uses one or the other of the white balls for his or her cue ball.

Balls are shot with a carom billiards cue, a thin wooden stick similar to a standard English billiards cue.

Carom billiards table

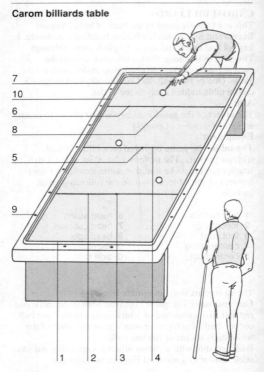

Order of play

Lots are usually drawn if there are more than two players.

When there are only two players or two teams, the order is decided by 'lagging'. In lagging, the red ball is placed on the foot spot. Each player then plays, on either side of the red ball, a cue ball from behind the head string, trying to hit the ball so that it bounces off the foot cushion. The player whose cue ball comes to rest nearest to the head cushion plays first.

Lagging

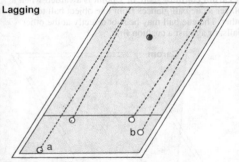

Player **a** plays first.

A lag is lost if a player's cue ball touches the red ball or interferes with an opponent's ball.

In the result of a tie or both players fouling, the lag is continued until the playing order is decided.

Playing

The break shot At the start of a game the red ball is placed on the foot spot and the white object ball is placed on the head spot. The cue ball is played from the head string, within 15cm (6in) – centre to centre – of the white object ball.

In a break shot, the cue ball must hit the red ball first. Other than on a break shot, a player's ball may hit either of the object balls first. A player continues to play until he or she fails to score.

A carom count or score of 1 point is awarded when a player's cue ball glances from one object ball to the other. The cue ball may be shot directly at the other balls, or against a cushion first.

Carom

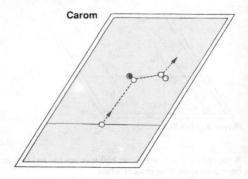

The safety shot allows a player to end his or her turn without a penalty.

Either the cue ball must come to rest against a cushion, after striking an object ball, or it must hit an object ball up against a cushion.

If the safety shot is not successful, the player loses a point.

When returning to the table for a turn, a player must make a serious attempt to score from the position left by the opponent's safety shot. If not, it is a foul with a 1-point penalty and the loss of the turn.

Safety shot

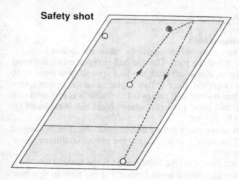

Jumped ball

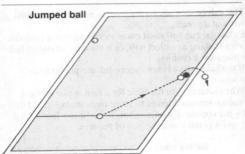

Jumped balls

When a cue ball is hit off the table, the striker loses 1 point and the turn. The cue ball is replaced on the head spot or, if it is covered, the foot spot. If both these spots are occupied, the cue ball is placed on the centre spot. When the red ball jumps off the table it is replaced onto the foot spot; a jumped white object ball is replaced on the head spot.

The score made before one or both object balls jumped off the table is counted, and the player continues his or her turn.

It is a foul if all the balls jump off the table. The offending player loses 1 point and the turn. In this case, as all the balls are replaced to the starting position, the incoming player must make a break shot.

If the cue ball bounces onto the rail and returns to the table it remains in play. If it stays on the rail, it is treated as a jumped ball.

Frozen balls

These are balls that are touching each other or a cushion. Frozen object balls remain in play as they are. If the cue ball is frozen, the player may shoot away from the frozen object ball or have the balls replaced for a break shot. Not to do either of these things is a foul, resulting in the loss of 1 point and the turn.

A cue ball frozen against a cushion may be played against that cushion first.

Fouls

All fouls result in the loss of 1 point and the end of the offending player's turn. In addition to the fouls described above (under **Jumping balls** and **Frozen balls**), the following are foul shots:

a playing a shot when any ball is still moving;

b touching the cue ball inadvertently while preparing for a shot;

c letting the cue tip remain in contact with the cue ball after the cue ball has struck an object ball;

d touching an object ball with the cue;

e playing the wrong cue ball; and

f having at least one foot off the floor while making a shot.

Winning the game

The first player to reach the previously agreed number of points, after deducting penalty points for foul shots, wins the game.

DOMINOES

Games with dominoes are played in many countries all over the world. It is thought that dominoes may have been brought to Europe from China in the 14th century. The modern game played in Britain developed in Italy; this version is very different from the Chinese one. Next to darts, dominoes is probably the most popular British pub game. In many pubs where dominoes is played seriously, one corner of the pub is set aside with a special table that has ridged edges to keep the dominoes from falling on the floor.

Aim

There are many domino games; in most, players try to add dominoes to a layout formed in the centre of the table.

The dominoes

These are rectangular tiles made of wood, ivory, bone, stone or plastic. They are sometimes also called 'bones', 'stones', or 'pieces'. The standard size is 2.5cm x 4cm x 1cm (1in x 1.9in x 0.4in).

Each domino face is divided in half by a central line; each half is either blank or marked with indented spots (sometimes called 'pips'). Dominoes with the same number of spots on either side of the central line are called 'doubles' or 'doublets'.

A domino is said to be 'heavier' than another if it has more spots, or 'lighter' if it has fewer spot. A double 6, for example, is heavier than 6:5.

The standard domino set has 28 tiles (with double 6 the heaviest domino). Larger sets have 55 dominoes (with double 9 the heaviest) or 91 dominoes (with double 12 the heaviest).

The complete standard domino set

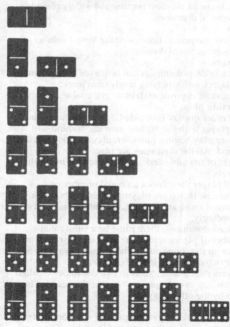

VARIATION: BLOCK/DRAW DOMINOES

This is one of the most popular and widely played versions of dominoes.

Aim

Players compete to finish with the lowest number of spots on unplayed dominoes.

Players

Block or draw dominoes can be played by any number of players, either playing singly or in pairs.

Partners sit opposite each other at the table.

Starting play

The order of play is decided by a preliminary draw; the player with the highest-ranking domino will start. Before play begins, however, players first each draw a hand. All the dominoes are placed face down in the centre of the table and are then shuffled by all the players.

Each player then draws an equal number of dominoes. If two are playing, each draws seven pieces; if more are playing, the number is reduced accordingly.

In draw dominoes, there must be a substantial number of pieces remaining after the first draw to make up the 'boneyard'. There must always be at least two dominoes in the boneyard.

Players then arrange their drawn dominoes – called 'hands', as in card games – so that they cannot be seen by the other players.

Playing

The first player begins by placing any domino from his or her hand in the centre of the table. The next player must play a domino with an end matching one

of the first domino's ends, then the next player does
the same, and so on.

Doubles are placed sideways in the layout; playing a
double earns the player an extra turn.

Blocking

Skill is needed in deciding which domino to play
when several are possible.

Players can 'block' their opponents' moves by
playing an 'unmatchable' domino. In block domino,
when this happens the blocked player loses his or her
turn. In draw domino, blocked players draw pieces
from the boneyard until they are able to play.

Ending the game

The game ends when one player has played all his or
her dominoes and calls 'domino!', or when no player
can add a matching domino from his or her hand and
only two dominoes remain in the boneyard.

Scoring

If a player wins by playing all his or her dominoes,
that player claims 1 point for each spot on the
opponent's unplayed dominoes.

If all play is blocked, the player with the fewest spots
on unplayed dominoes claims the difference between
the number of spots on his or her own and those on
the opponents' unplayed dominoes. The hand is
replayed if the opponent's dominoes have an equal
number of spots.

ENGLISH BILLIARDS

Some English pubs still have English billiards tables, although they have been replaced by pool tables in many places. English billiards tables can be found in many northern pubs, while the bar billiards table (see p.67) remains prevalent in southern pubs.

Aim

English billiards is played by two players or four playing in two teams. Three balls are used: a white, a spot white and a red. The object is to score points by pocketing balls (called a 'hazard') or by striking the other balls (called a 'cannon').

Equipment

The table The standard table is 3.6m x 1.9m (12ft x 6.1ft); smaller tables are sometimes used. The elements of the table are as follows:

1 the spot	**7** the baulk
2 pyramid spot	**8** bottom pocket
3 centre spot	**9** centre pocket
4 baulk line	**10** top pocket
5 baulk line spot	**11** cushion
6 the D	

The cues and rest Billiard cues are narrow wooden sticks; they come in varying sizes, but are no less than 91cm (3ft) long.

All billiards tables are equipped with a full-length cue 2.8m (9ft) long, a half cue 2.1m (7ft) long, a rest 2.4m (8ft) long and a half rest 1.5 (5ft) long.

The rests are used to support the cue for a shot beyond a player's reach.

The balls The white ball and the spot white are cue

The English billiards table

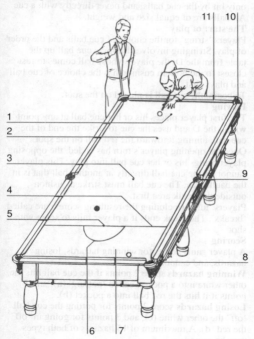

balls, one used by each player (or pair). The red ball is only hit by the cue balls, and never directly with a cue. All balls are of equal size and weight.

The start of play

Players 'string' for the choice of cue balls and the order of play. Stringing involves hitting a cue ball up the table from the D; the player whose ball comes to rest closest to the bottom cushion has the choice of cue ball and plays first.

To begin, the red ball is placed on the spot.

Playing

The first player places his or her cue ball at any point within the D and uses the cue to strike the end of the cue ball, aiming it toward the red ball on the spot.

Once the opening player's turn has ended, the opposing player brings his or her cue ball into play. This player cannot hit the cue ball directly at another ball that is in the baulk area. The cue ball must strike a cushion outside the baulk area first.

Players' turns (including the resulting scores) are called 'breaks'. The break ends if a player fails to score with a shot.

Scoring

A player gains points for winning hazards, losing hazards, and cannons.

Winning hazards score 2 points if the cue ball hits the other white into a pocket, called 'potting' (**a**); and 3 points if it hits the red ball into a pocket (**b**).

Losing hazards score 2 points for potting the cue ball 'off' the other white (**c**), and 3 points for going in 'off' the red (**d**). A maximum of 15 hazards of both types may be scored.

Hazards

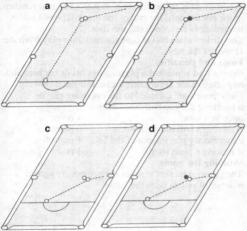

Cannons score 2 points if the cue ball strikes both the other balls. If the cue ball is potted, an extra 2 points are scored if the other white was hit first, and an extra 3 if the red was hit first before going in.

Touching balls

When a player's ball comes to rest against another ball, the red ball is replaced onto the spot. If the non-striker's ball is on the table, it is replaced on the centre spot; if not the player plays from the D.

Potted balls

When a ball is potted, the non-striker's cue ball remains in the pocket until the end of the break. The red ball is immediately replaced onto the spot.

The striker's cue ball is brought back into play from the D area of the table.

Fouls and penalties

Once a foul is made the player loses his or her turn and any score made during that break. For the following fouls, points are awarded to the opposing player:

a touching the cue ball more than

once in a shot: 1 point

b forcing a ball off the table: 3 points

c incorrectly playing out of the D: 1 point

d making a push shot: 1 point

Winning the game

The player who first reaches the previously agreed number of points wins the game.

HOOD SKITTLES

This game is similar to the larger-scale floor version, Old English skittles (see p.24), but is played on a special table.

Several leagues in the East Midlands call the game table skittles, Northants skittles or Leicester skittles. There are as many variations in the rules as there are leagues, so the details given here are a summary of the most common form of hood skittles.

Equipment

The table Sometimes called the board, the table is rather like an elongated armchair because the sides and back of the table are surrounded by padded arms which form a hood from which the 'cheeses' can rebound as they are thrown.

A net at the back catches stray, or 'flying', cheeses. The table surface itself is flat with a diamond-shaped area at the back on which the skittles stand.

The player stands 2.1–2.4m (7–8ft) away from the table to throw.

Skittles There are nine wooden skittles, known as 'pins'. They have the same tubby shape as the larger ones used in Old English skittles, but are only 12.6cm (5in) high. Some leagues prefer to use plastic pins.

Cheeses The aim is to knock the pins down with 'cheeses', missiles shaped like round Dutch cheeses. The cheeses are 7.6cm (3in) in diameter and 3.8cm (1.5in) thick. Flat on top and bottom, their edges are rounded so the whole thing fits well into the hand for an underarm throw. The cheese can be aimed directly at the pins or thrown to rebound off the padded sides of the table.

Playing

There are generally eight players to a team, with each player paired with one from the opposing team. Each pair plays a series of singles games until one loses.

Pairs toss a coin for the first throw. The two players each throw three cheeses in turn.

If a player throws a 'floorer' (all pins down with one cheese) or a 'stack' (all pins down with two cheeses) the pins are reset.

Losing lives

Each player is said to have five lives. When both have thrown their three cheeses, the one with the worse score loses one life.

Scores are the total number of pins knocked down during the three throws.

The player who is first to lose all five lives loses the singles contest.

VARIATION: KILLER SKITTLES

This is a variation for any number of players, sometimes played for a small stake – such as 10p in the pot from each player.

After deciding the order of play by tossing a coin, the first player throws with his or her unfamiliar hand, i.e. left-handed if normally a right-handed person. The next player in turn must knock down a greater number of pins than the previous player; otherwise, the next player loses a life. Then the following player must knock down more pins than the last best score, and so on. The pins are reset each time, and the player's score is recorded.

Each player has an equal number of lives – three or five, as agreed.

The next round

At the end of the first round, the second player in the
first round becomes first player and throws with his or
her unfamiliar hand to establish the number of pins to
be exceeded. The players continue in the same order as
before, but the previous starting player throws last.
The rounds continue. When a player has lost all three
(or five) lives, he or she drops out. The last remaining
player is the winner and collects the pot.

The hood skittles table

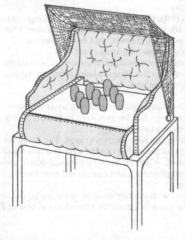

VARIATION: DADDLUMS

This is a variation of table or hood skittles that used to be found in the southeast of England. The Vigo Inn near Seven Oaks in Kent still has a daddlums table.

Equipment

The daddlums table is longer and narrower than the hood skittles table. In general the table is 1.7m (5.5ft) long. Although the sides and back are quite high, they are not padded.

The pins are only 7.6cm (3in) high and the cheeses are lightweight and small, about 5cm (2in) in diameter.

Technique

At 2.7m (9ft), the throwing distance is longer than for hood skittles. This, together with the narrower table and smaller pins and cheeses, makes daddlums a challenging game requiring great skill.

Rebounds are not used and the method is to throw in such a way that the cheese slides along the table to knock down the pins.

Playing

Any of the skittles games can be played on the daddlums table, but the one used in Kent is a game of nines between two players.

Each player has nine throws in turn. The score for the turn is the total number of pins knocked down with the nine throws. When all the nine pins are down, they are reset if the player has not completed nine throws.

Winning

The player with the higher score wins the round, or 'leg'. The game is generally played to the best of five legs.

A daddlums table

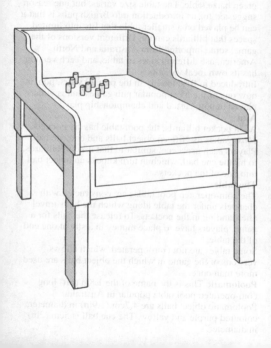

POOL

Pool is a derivative of billiards, played on a smaller green baize table. The table size varies, but one reason suggested for its introduction into British pubs is that it can be played on a smaller table that fits into limited spaces that billiards cannot. Different versions of the game, some imported from Australia and North America, use different sizes of table, and each version has its own local variations.

Introduced in Britain only in the past 20 years, pool is now one of the most popular pub games and is widely played in both casual and championship play.

Aim

As in pocket billiards, the pool table has six pockets. Most games use fifteen object balls and one cue ball. Players each use a cue, similar to that used in billiards, to hit the cue ball, which in turn knocks an object ball into one of the pockets.

The table

The coin-operated pool tables are constructed with channels under the table along which the balls travel after landing in the pockets. To release the balls for a game, players have to place money in a slot at one end of the table.

Some tables are not coin-operated, which allows versions of the game in which the object balls are used more than once.

Poolomatic This is the name of the 1.8m (6ft) long coin-operated pool table popular in Australia. Poolomatic object balls are 4.7cm (1.9in) in diameter, coloured purple and yellow. The cue ball is 5cm (2in) in diameter.

American pool table

North American pool The American table is 2.7m (9ft) long, three quarters the size of a standard billiards/snooker table. The four corner pockets are 1.2cm (0.5in) narrower in diameter than the two side pockets.

The standard British table Although tables come in all sizes, to fit the average pub, the British Association of Pool Table Operators agreed the size of a standard table as 2.1m (7ft) long and 1m (3.5ft) wide.

The table also has a D-ring marked on the baulk line.

Other shapes

Some odd-shaped tables were manufactured from time to time. For example, a pub in Baydon, Oxfordshire, had a hexagonal table made in the early 1990s to fit the only space available in a corner. The table can be turned to play different shots, a manoeuvre requiring care to prevent the balls rolling about.

Whatever size it is, the table is set up as shown on the previous page. The cue ball starts from any position on the baulk line.

Pool balls

There are fifteen object balls, each numbered. Balls 1 to 8 are solid colours, number 8 being black; balls 9 to 15 are striped.

Balls used in pool

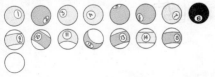

Alternatively, there may be seven yellow and seven red balls, plus one black ball.

In addition, there is a single white cue ball used by all players.

The object balls are 5cm (2in) in diameter, and the cue ball is somewhat narrower – 4.7cm (1.8in).

VARIATION: STRAIGHT POOL

Also known as 14.1 continuous, this is the American game seen played by Paul Newman in the film *The Hustler*.

The balls are racked, i.e. set in a starting triangle by the use of a triangular frame. The ball at one corner is placed over the foot spot on the table. The cue ball is 'spotted' – i.e. placed on the baulk line – for the first shot.

Players toss a coin for first play. The first player aims to hit the cue ball into an object ball and to pocket the object balls (called 'potting'), one after another in any order, until only one object ball is left.

If the player does this without missing a pot, he or she continues the break by racking all fifteen balls and attempting to pot fourteen of them again.

When the first player fails to pot a ball, the opponent takes over, using the balls as they were left by the first player. This player also has the opportunity for a second racking.

Each pot scores 1 point, and play continues until an agreed time.

British version of straight pool

This game, often used for major contests, is sometimes played in one room while players await the results in another room. Also, it can be played along with other games. A time limit is determined before play begins. An entry fee of £1 per player can be charged, for which participants can play as many games as they wish within the time limit.

A player's name and score remain on a blackboard until his or her score is exceeded by another player. It is therefore easy to see the highest score, and who is winning, at any time.

When time is up, the winner is the player with the highest score, as on the blackboard. The winner then collects all the entry fees as the prize.

VARIATION: EIGHT-BALL POOL

This is the most popular pool game played in Britain. Usually played between two singles, teams can also compete by players pairing up with each other for a singles game.

The balls are racked with the black (8) ball at the centre and a striped and a coloured ball, respectively, in each of the bottom corners. All other balls can be placed anywhere in the rack.

The rack ready for an eight-ball game

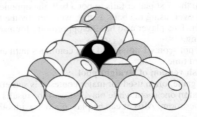

Playing

After the toss for order of play, the rack is removed and the first player aims to pot either of the two numerical sequences, 1 to 7 or 9 to 15, in any order, and finally the black 8.

Which numerical sequence a player must pot is decided by the first ball potted. If it is a striped ball, the player must pot another striped ball, but in any order.

To continue the turn, or 'break', a player must either pot a ball or hit the cushion with any two balls. When a player fails to do either, the break ends and the opponent plays.

The opponent aims to pot the other set of balls, i.e. the coloured set in this example.

Play continues alternately until one player has potted all his or her seven balls, followed by the black ball, winning that game.

Scratching

If the cue ball is accidentally potted, it is called a 'scratch'. Coin-operated tables are designed to return the cue ball, which is somewhat smaller than the other balls, through a narrower channel. On other tables, the cue ball is simply retrieved from the pocket. In both cases, the player who scratched loses his or her turn, the cue ball is spotted on the baulk line, and the opponent takes over.

In some rules a scratch counts as a foul, giving the opposing player an extra turn.

Calling pockets

American pool rules require players to 'call' pockets – that is, to state which pocket they are aiming for. In some games, calling is only required on the last shot –

i.e. the 8 ball. If a player fails to pocket a ball in the called pocket, his or her turn ends.

Calling pockets is usually not required by British rules.

Fouls

A foul gives the opponent an extra shot. Fouls are:

1 potting a ball off any other ball (besides the black, which loses the game);

2 jumping the cue ball over another ball;

3 failing to hit any ball with the cue ball; and

4 not having both feet on the ground.

Automatic loss

If a player pots the black ball before potting all his or her other balls, that player automatically loses the game. Also, a player who pots a ball off the black ball loses the game.

In some games, especially those played by American rules, a player who, after potting all his or her other balls, aims for the black ball and misses it, loses the game.

VARIATION: NINE-BALL POOL

This variation is played in America, Germany, Sweden and some other European countries, although it is not as popular in Britain. It can be played on a standard British coin-operated table.

Only nine balls are used. Balls numbered 1 to 9 are racked in a diamond shape with the 1 at the top facing the baulk line and the 9 at the centre. Numbers 2 to 8 can be anywhere in the diamond.

The aim is to pocket the 9 but the 1 must be hit first. Otherwise, the game proceeds as eight-ball pool except that if a player makes a foul shot, the balls are re-racked for the opponent to begin the game again.

The rack ready for a nine-ball game

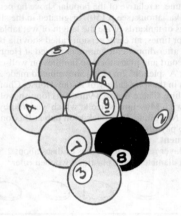

SHOVELBOARD

This game, a relative of the popular shove ha'penny and its variations (see p.150), originated in the sliding of mugs or tankards of ale the length of wet tables. In Tudor times, an early version called shovilla bourde was an after-dinner entertainment played at Henry VIII's court and in aristocratic families on well-crafted boards. A splendid 7m (23ft) shovelboard made about 1570 is in the long gallery of Astley House, Chorley, Lancashire. There is also a 9m (30ft) long shovelboard in Norwich Museum, Norfolk, which was sold by an Earl of Norfolk to The Black Lion pub at Buxton in 1732 to pay off debts.

Equipment

Each player requires four coins or discs about 2.5cm (1in) in diameter and a plastic or wooden ruler.

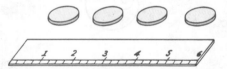

Each player's equipment

In medieval times the shovelboard tables were long and narrow – perhaps 9m (30ft) long. The higher scoring area extended 10cm (4in) from the table's end and the lower scoring area 122cm (4ft) in front of that.

It is possible, however, to play a form of shovelboard on almost any rectangular or square table by marking off an out-of-play area and scaling down the dimensions of the scoring areas.

Players

Shovelboard is a game for two players or two teams of
equal number.

In team games, each player normally plays a round
against an opponent from the other team. The two
opponents in a round propel one coin alternately.

Playing

In turn, players shoot one of their coins toward the
scoring area. Players shoot using their rulers to give the
coin a push.

All coins, except those more than halfway over the out-
of-play lines, are left on the table until the end of the
round. This makes hitting one coin into another an
important feature of the game.

Scoring

Players score:

a 3 points for any coin partly over the edge of the table;

b 2 points for any coin completely in the far scoring
area;

c 1 point for any coin completely in the near scoring
area; and

d 1 point for any coin on the line between the near and
far scoring areas.

Winning the game

In singles games, the winner is the first person to score
an agreed number of points – such as 11.

Team games can be decided in several ways:

1 the team winning the most rounds;

2 the team with the most points after an agreed number
of rounds; or

3 the first team to score an agreed number of points.

SHUFFLEBOARD

Shuffleboard descended from shovelboard (see p.98), which went into a decline among the aristocracy for several hundred years but re-emerged in Californian bars in the early 20th century, where it was played on the ground rather than on a table and became a popular game on the decks of cruise ships. The game described here is this version but played on a special table; it varies from the original shovelboard, which is rarely played today. In Britain, shuffleboard is now played at The Brunswick pub in Hove, Sussex, and at the Ship Inn, East Grinstead, Suffolk.

Aim

Players attempt to score points by propelling discs or weights along a table into marked scoring areas.

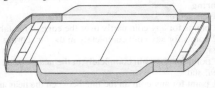

Equipment

Each player or team has four heavy weights made of metal. These should be about 2.5cm (1in) in diameter. An official shuffleboard table is 3.6m x 0.9m (12ft x 3ft) and about 0.9m (3ft) high. The surface is very smooth, like glass. At each end is a u-shaped area known as the 'gutter' in which overshot discs fall. On either side of the board is a cushion, like that on a billiards table, off which the discs must bounce when played.

The table has several important markings: a central foul line divides the table in half, and at either end are areas marked with scores of 1, 2, 3 and 5.

Players

The game can be played by two players competing (singles game) or four players in two teams. In a singles game, both players shoot from one end of the table; in team games players sit or stand at opposite ends.

Playing

Players toss a coin for first shot.

When shot, the weight must bounce off a cushion and must pass the central foul line; otherwise, it is considered 'dead' and is removed.

Then the next player shoots, and so on until all weights have been played.

Scoring

The points value for each player's or team's weights is calculated, based on the scoring areas where they landed. The player with the highest-value shot earns the points for that weight as well as those for any of his or her weights that scored higher than the opponent's.

A weight resting on a line between two scoring areas earns the lower value of the two.

A 'scoring hanger' is when a weight overhangs the edge of the table in the 3-point or 5-point areas. A scoring hanger earns 1 bonus point.

Winning the game

The winner of the round is the player with the highest score. A game consists of as many rounds as are needed for one player to reach 15 points, in a singles game; or 21 points in a team game.

SNOOKER

Snooker is a combination of several older games: pyramid, black pool and life pool. It originated in India, and was probably brought to Britain in the late 19th century by professional billiards player John Roberts. The game eventually overtook billiards in popularity, although for some reason it remains a uniquely British game and is little played elsewhere.

Equipment

Table The full-size snooker table is the same as a billiards table, with six pockets, but many pubs have three-quarter or half-size tables.

Balls There are 22 balls of equal size and weight: one white cue ball and 21 balls of different colours and worth points when pocketed, as follows:

15 red:	1 point
1 yellow:	2 points
1 green:	3 points
1 brown:	4 points
1 blue:	5 points
1 pink:	6 points
1 black:	7 points

In the game of snooker plus, there are also an orange ball (worth 8 points) and a purple ball (worth 10 points). Although this game is rarely played anymore, there are reminders of it in the stray orange and purple balls found with some pubs' snooker tables.

Cue Players use a billiards cue to strike the balls.

Aim

Players try to score points by pocketing, or 'potting', balls and to force opponents to lose points by 'snookering' them (see **Snookering** on p.105).

Playing

Players toss a coin to determine playing order, and the cue ball is 'spotted' – i.e. placed anywhere with the D on the table – for the first shot. The other balls are placed on the table as shown; a triangular rack is used for the red balls.

Location of balls for snooker

Y = yellow
G = green
BR = brown
BL = blue
P = pink
BK - black

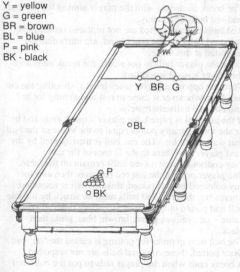

The initial shot must strike the cue ball against a red ball. If a player pots a red, he or she earns 1 point and continues the turn, called the 'break', by trying to pot any non-red ball. The ball aimed for must be 'called' – that is, the player must state which ball he or she is trying to strike with the cue ball. Any balls that are potted earn the player the points shown in the points table on p.102.

The break continues with the player aiming for red and non-red balls alternately.

Red balls that are potted are not replaced on the table; coloured balls, on the other hand, are immediatedy respotted at this stage.

Once the player fails to pot a ball, the break ends and the player's score is totalled.

Then the opposing player takes breaks, shooting the cue ball from wherever it came to rest and aiming for red and non-red balls alternately.

If the cue ball is potted, the player's break ends and he or she loses penalty points equal to the value of the ball that was aimed for. The cue ball is then spotted by the next player anywhere in the D area of the table.

Play continues until no red balls remain on the table. The player potting the last red ball may then aim for any coloured ball. If potted, this last ball is respotted. Thereafter, the coloured balls must be struck by the cue ball and potted only in strict ascending order of point value – i.e., yellow, green, brown, blue, pink, then black.

The ball next in order for potting is called the 'on' ball. Once potted, these coloured balls are not respotted.

A break ends when the player fails to pot the coloured

ball of lowest value left on the table.

Snookering

A player is 'snookered' when a ball that is not the on ball is obstructing a straight line between the cue ball and the on ball. The player must nevertheless attempt to hit the on ball; missing it loses the player penalty points worth the value of the on ball.

A snooker

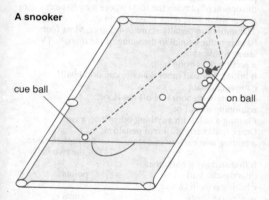

cue ball

on ball

Balls touching

If the cue ball comes to rest against another ball, it must be played away from that ball without moving it. If it is moved in the shot, it counts as a penalty, losing the player either the value of the ball moved or the value of the on ball, whichever is greater. If the ball touching the cue ball is the on ball, no penalty applies.

Fouls and penalties

A shot earning a penalty is called a 'foul'. After a foul shot, such as an unsuccessful recovery from a snooker or a touching ball, the striker's break ends and he or she loses any points earned in that break. The penalty points applying are credited to the opponent, who has the option of playing the balls where they have come to rest or asking the other player to do so.

The minimum penalty score is 4 points. Most fouls have penalties equal to the value of the on ball. These are as follows:

a potting the wrong ball;

b hitting any ball other than the cue or on ball;

c moving a ball;

d playing with both feet off the floor;

e jumping a ball; or

f hitting a ball with anything other than a cue.

Other fouls carry different penalties:

a potting two balls in one shot:　　the higher value
　　　　　　　　　　　　　　　　　of the two balls

b first striking a ball other
than the cue ball:　　　　　　　7 points

c hitting reds in two or more
successive shots:　　　　　　　7 points

Ending the game

The game ends once all balls are potted. The players' scores are then totalled, subtracting any penalty points against players and crediting them to their opponents. The player with the highest score is the winner.

SQUAILS

Squails is a type of table bowls that was popular in Britain in the last century. Although not widely played today, it is an easy-to-learn game for any number of players using improvised equipment – and so is a good pub game.

Aim

Players are divided into two teams and seek to position small discs, called 'squails', as near as possible to a metal target placed on the table.

Equipment

Squails can be played on any kind of table, but a fairly strong, round one is best. The game was originally played with wooden discs about 3.8cm (1.5in) in diameter and raised at the centre. Any similar-size discs can be used as squails – such as coins, coasters or plastic tiddlywinks.

Each player has an equal number of squails, and each team's squails should be clearly differentiated by colour or by number.

Targets, also called 'processes' or 'jacks', are usually made of metal and can be any size, although they should be quite heavy. A small medal or lead cylinder can be used.

The target is placed in the centre of the table at the start of a round.

Players

Squails is a game for any even number of players, but four to eight is probably best.

Players are divided into two teams, and team members take alternate places around the table.

Playing

Choice of playing order goes to the player who shoots his or her squail nearest the target in a preliminary play. Then, in turn, each player places his or her squail partly over the edge of the table and pushes it with the palm of the hand, aiming for the target.

Turns pass clockwise around the table, alternating between teams.

Playing one squail into another to move it toward or away from the target is permitted.

If a squail pushes the target more than 15cm (6in) away from the centre of the table, the target must be put back in its original position.

A squail that goes off the table or stops within 7.5cm (3in) of the table edge is considered dead for the round.

Scoring

Points are scored after all players have played all their squails for a round.

The squail farthest from the target scores 1 point, next farthest 2 points, and so on to the squail nearest the target.

A team scores an additional 2 points if during the round a player on the opposing team knocks the target off the table or within 7.5cm (3in) of the table edge.

Winning the game

The winning team is the one with the highest score after an agreed number of rounds.

TOAD-IN-THE-HOLE

An early version of toad-in-the-hole was a 16th-century game played on the hills by shepherds. They aimed to throw stones into selected holes and hollows, pitching uphill. It is thought the shepherds brought the game into inns they visited after work, such as The Ram Inn at Firle, The Anchor at Ringmer and The Fountain Inn at Plumpton Green, all in Sussex, England.

The game also exists in a few East Anglian pubs where the table on which it is played was originally built into the pub furniture, and was thus preservedthrough the years.

Equipment

Four brass counters are needed – these are known as 'toads'. They can be any weight from 28–85gm (1–3oz). Like coins, they have two distinguishable sides.

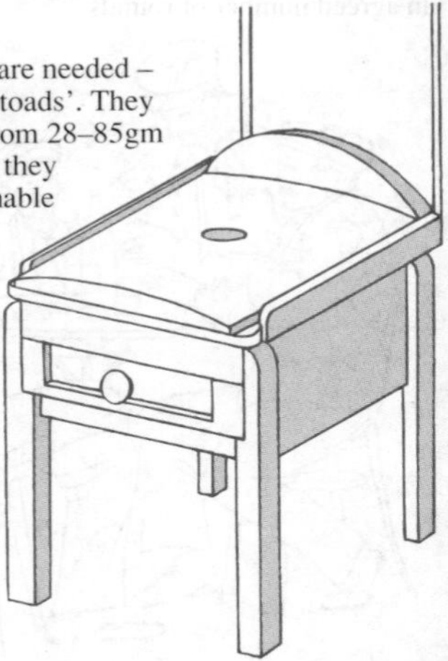

A toad-in-the-hole table is sturdy, about 91cm (3ft) long and 46cm (18in) wide, although some are square.

The top, called the 'roof', is covered with a layer of a soft lead in which there is a central hole through which the toads fall. Beneath is a drawer to catch the toads.

On some tables there is a retaining board along the back edge which prevents the unskilled from pitching their toads across the room or hitting a wall.

Playing

The player stands on a line marked 2.4m (8ft) away from the table and throws the toad. The aim is to get it into the hole or to make a top-shot by landing it on the roof of the table without any sliding.

The game

Two players agree on a winning score of either 31 or 61 points. They toss a coin, or a toad, to decide who goes first.

The first player throws two toads, one after the other. The opposing player follows with three toads. Then the players continue throws, each using all four toads in each turn, until one player reaches the winning number.

Scoring

A toad thrown exactly in the hole scores 2 points. One that lands on the roof, and stays put, scores 1 point.

There is no score if a toad:

a does not land on the roof;

b slides on the roof before coming to rest; or

c hits the backboard before coming to rest, even if it rebounds into the hole.

A cribbage scoring board is useful for scoring, or a non-player can keep a reckoning.

If a player has either 30 or 60 points and scores another 2 by getting a toad in the hole, the 2 does not count. A player wins only when the winning number is reached exactly.

3. Board games

BACKGAMMON

Descended from an ancient Persian game called nard, backgammon became popular throughout Europe in the 17th century. The French called it tric-trac, the Spanish tablas reales and in Italy it was tavole real. Puff was the German name, gammon the Scots name and in England it was known as backgammon. Innkeepers provided the game for travellers, and it was often recommended as a cure for the gout and other painful afflictions. Backgammon is played at The Six Bells in Lincolnshire.

Equipment

Each player has fifteen pieces, also known as 'counters' or 'stones'. The counters are of bone or plastic and are identical except for colour. One player has dark counters and is known as 'Black'; the other has light-coloured counters and is known as 'White'.

Each player also has two dice and a cup in which to shake them.

The game is played on a rectangular board divided into two by a bar. One half of the board is called the 'inner table' or 'home table'; the other is the 'outer table'.

Aim

Two players compete. According to the numbers thrown on the dice, each player moves his or her counters toward the inner table on his or her side. Once a player's counters are all in the inner table, the player attempts to remove them by a process called 'bearing off'. The first player to bear off all of his or her fifteen pieces wins the game.

Along each side of the board are marked twelve triangles, alternately light and dark coloured (this colouring has no special significance). Each triangle is called a 'point'. For the purpose of notation, points are numbered 1–12 as shown. (No numbers actually appear on the board.) Points 1 (the first points in the inner

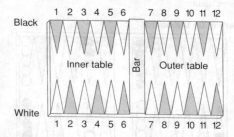

table) are called 'ace points'; points 7 (the first points on the outer table) are called 'bar points'. No other points are specially designated.

The board is placed between the two players so that Black has the inner table to his or her right. The points on Black's side of the table are known as Black points; those on White's side are White points. In simple notation, points are indicated by their number and the initial B or W.

Starting play

Players draw for colour and then place their counters in their prescribed starting positions. White places two counters on B1, five on W6, three on W8 and five on

B12. Black places two counters on W1, five on B6, three on B8 and five on W12.

Having placed their counters in their starting positions, each player throws a single die to determine the order of play. The player throwing the higher number has first move. If both players throw the same number they must throw again.

Setting up the board

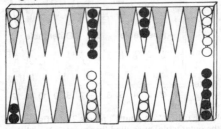

For the first move the opening player moves according to the numbers on both his or her own and the opponent's dice. Thereafter, play alternates and each player moves according to the numbers on both his or her own dice.

The direction of play for each player is always from the opponent's inner table, through the opponent's outer table, through his or her own outer table, and into his or her own inner table. Thus White always moves counters in a clockwise direction and Black always moves counterclockwise.

Playing

In turn, players throw both their dice to determine how many points to move. For a valid throw the dice must be thrown from the cup in the player's own half of the board. The dice are thrown only when the opponent's turn has finished, and they must land so that one face of each die rests wholly on the board.

The player then moves according to the numbers thrown on the dice.

When moving counters, players may not simply move the number of points indicated by the combined total of the dice. Each die must represent a separate move. The position of the counters on the board may affect a player's choice of moves or may even prevent the player from moving at all.

Provided that none of his or her counters is off the board, a player may land on any point that is:

a clear of any other counters;

b occupied by one or more of his or her own counters; or

c occupied by only one of the opponent's counters.

Moving counters

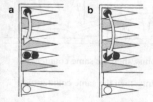

'Taking' counters When there is only one counter on a point, it is called a 'blot'. The opponent can land on this point and 'take' the single counter, placing it on the central bar dividing the board. The player whose piece is so taken cannot move again until he or she throws the exact number needed to move this counter to an unblocked point.

A player who moves a counter to a point on which he or she already has one counter is said to 'make' that point, as the opponent cannot then land on it.

Mixed throw If the numbers on the two dice are different, it is called a 'mixed throw', and the player may make one of four possible moves. For example, a player throwing a 2 and a 6 may move:

Mixed throw moves

a

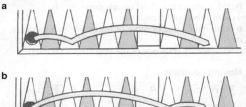

b

a one counter two points, then the same counter six points further;
b one counter six points, then the same counter two points further;

c one counter two points, and another counter six points;

d one counter six points, and another counter two points.

Mixed throw moves (cont.)

c

d

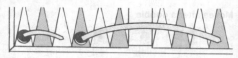

At first glance, alternatives **a** and **b** appear to be the same. This is not in fact the case, since the order in which the numbers are taken can effect whether or not a counter may be moved. If two opponent's counters are already on a point two points away, for example, the player cannot make move **a** but can possibly make move **b**.

If a player can use only the number shown on one of the dice, the other number is disregarded. If one of the two numbers can be used, the player must use the higher one.

A double If a player throws a double, such as two 2s, then the number shown on both dice is played four times (or as many times as possible up to four). Thus, a player throwing two 2s may move:

a one counter four times two points;
b one counter twice two points and another counter twice two points;
c one counter twice two points and another two counters two points each; or
d four counters two points each.

Moves after a double

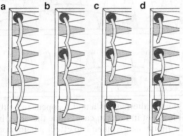

As before, the number shown on the dice is the limit of a move. A player moving one counter four times two points must land on open points at the end of each two-point move.

Bearing off Once players succeed in moving all their counters into their own inner table, they 'bear them off' by removing them from those points (1–6) that correspond to the numbers thrown. For example, if White throws a 4 and a 2 and has counters on both W4 and W2, he or she may bear off a counter from each of these points.

If White throws a 4 and a 2 and has a counter on W4 but not on W2, the player may bear off a counter from W4 and must then move another counter two points down from the highest occupied point. If desired, a player may always move counters down the board from the highest point rather than bearing off from the points corresponding to the numbers on the dice.

If both numbers thrown are higher than the player's highest point, the player bears off from the highest point.

If a player's counter is taken after he or she has started bearing off, that counter must be re-entered as described above and moved around again to the inner table before bearing off is resumed.

Bearing off continues until one player succeeds in bearing off all his or her counters.

Winning the game

The game is won by the player who first bears off all his or her counters. The number of units scored depends on the progress of the loser, as in the following:

a If the loser has borne off at least one counter and has no counters left in the winner's inner table, the winner scores 1 point, or 'unit'.

b If the loser has not borne off any counters, the winner has made a 'gammon' and scores 2 units.

c If the loser has not borne off any counters and also has a counter on the bar or in the winner's inner table, the winner has made a 'backgammon' and scores 2 units.

CHESS

One of the oldest games in the world, originating in oriental cultures, chess was popular in the hostelries of Britain in the 15th century. The game played in the West is quite different from that played in the East.
In Britain, the game is now more likely to be found in country house hotels or cafes than in taverns and pubs, although a few schools and public parks provide large-scale outdoor 'boards' where play is with life-size chess pieces.
Although as played by professionals chess is highly complex and sophisticated, it can also be enjoyed at a simpler level by inexperienced players. It is a game of strategy for two people, with each piece – from the king to the pawn – representing units in an army.

The chess board

Equipment

The board is a large square divided into eight rows of eight squares each. The squares are alternately dark and light coloured (usually black and white).

The board is placed between facing players so that each has a white square at the right-hand corner.

The rows of squares running vertically between facing players are called 'files'; those running at right angles to the files are called 'ranks'. Rows of squares of the same colour that touch only at their corners are called 'diagonals'.

The pieces are positioned on the board at the start of the game. There are 32 in all: 16 are dark in colour, 16 light. They are called 'black' and 'white' respectively and make up the two sides.

A player's side is made up of six different kinds of pieces. These are, in descending order of importance: king, queen, rook (castle), bishop, knight, pawn. Each player has one king and one queen; two each of rooks, bishops and knights; and eight pawns.

Aim

The objective of each player is to capture the opponent's king. Unlike the other pieces, the king cannot be removed from the board; it is held to be captured when it has been 'checkmated'.

The player forcing checkmate wins the game – even if the pieces that player still has on the board are outnumbered by the opponent's pieces.

A player seeing the imminent checkmate of his or her king or recognising a losing situation will often resign. The player forcing the resignation then wins the game.

Moves

Each kind of piece can move a certain distance in one or more directions. Moves are limited by conditions on the board at the time of play.

A piece may move to any square within its range, provided that:

a the square is unoccupied by a piece of its own colour;

b if the square is occupied by an opponent's piece, that piece is first 'captured' and removed from the board; and

c it does not, with the exception of the knight's move, cross a square that is occupied by a piece of either colour.

The king is the most important piece on the board, and its capture by checkmate ends the game. It is represented diagrammatically by a crown.

The king can move one square in any direction, provided that this square is not one where it can be taken. Opposing kings can never stand on touching squares.

King's moves

 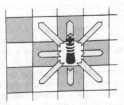

Castling The only time that a king may move more than one square is in a 'castling' move involving the rook. A player can make a castling move only once in a game.

The move is made to produce a defensive position around the king and to allow a rook to come into play. It comprises two stages, as follows:

1 moving the king two squares to the left or to the right from its original position and towards one of the rooks; then

2 transferring that rook to the square over which the king has just passed.

Castling

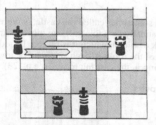

Castling is allowed provided that:

a neither the king nor the rook involved has moved from its original position;

b no piece of either colour is between the king and the rook involved in the castling move; and

c the square that the king must cross is not under attack by an opponent's piece.

The queen, represented diagrammatically by a coronet, is the most powerful attacking piece. It can move to any square on the rank, file or either of the two diagonals on which it is placed.

Queen's moves

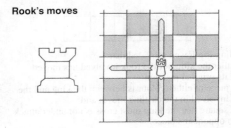

The rook, sometimes called the castle, is represented diagrammatically by a tower. It can move to any square on the rank or file on which it is placed. In addition, either one of the rooks in each side may be involved with the king in the castling move (see p.123).

Rook's moves

The bishop, represented by a mitre, moves to any square on the diagonal. Thus each player has one bishop that can move on a black diagonal and one on a white diagonal.

Bishop's moves

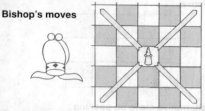

The knight is represented by a horse's head. In a single move it travels two squares in any direction along a rank or file and then one further square to the side. Thus whenever a knight moves from a black square it must land on a white square – and vice versa – on a different rank and file than where it started. In moving, a knight may cross a square occupied by any other piece; it is the only piece allowed to do so.

Knight's moves

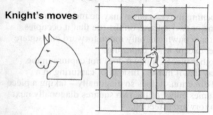

The pawn, represented diagrammatically by a small ball on a collared stem, has the most restricted movements of any piece: it can only move forwards.

Pawn's move

Pawn's alternative move on opening

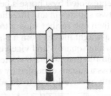

In its opening move, a pawn may be moved forward either one or two squares on the file that it occupies. Thereafter, a pawn can only move forward one square at a time, except when capturing.

Unlike other pieces, a pawn does not capture in the same way that it moves. Instead of capturing in a forward direction, it does so diagonally – taking a piece that occupies either of the two squares diagonally next to it in a forward direction.

Pawn capture

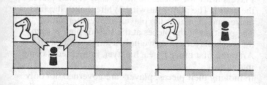

In addition, a pawn may capture an opposing pawn *'en passant'* (in passing). If the opposing pawn moves forward two squares in its opening move, the square it crosses is open to attack as though the pawn had only advanced one square. Thus the capturing pawn may take its usual taking move (i.e. one square diagonally forward) onto the square just crossed by the opposing pawn – the opposing pawn is then considered 'captured' and is removed from the board. (The *en passant* capture must be made as soon as the opposing pawn has moved forward two squares.)

Pawn promotion Whenever a pawn reaches the end of the file on which it is moving (i.e. it reaches the far side of the board) it must, in the same move, be exchanged for a queen, rook, bishop or knight – this is called 'promoting'. The choice of piece is made by the player promoting the pawn and is made without taking into account the number and kind of pieces on the board. Theoretically, therefore, a player could have up to nine queens on the board.

The 'promotion' takes effect immediately.

Playing

Players draw for sides, and then position their pieces on
the board. The player drawing White makes the first
move, and thereafter the players move alternately.
The position of the pieces at the start of play is such
that each player can move only a knight or a pawn.
After the first move by each player, more pieces come
into play.

In moving their pieces, players are governed not only
by the rules laid down for each piece but also the rules
that affect how pieces can be handled.

If a player touches a piece that can legitimately be
moved, then the piece must be moved unless the player
has warned that he or she is adjusting the piece on its
square. The usual warning used is '*J'adoube*' (I
adjust). Similarly, if a player touches an enemy piece
that can be taken, the touched piece must be captured
unless the player has given a prior warning.

Capturing move

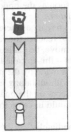
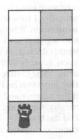

A move is completed when:

a a player's hand has left a piece after it has been moved to a vacant square;

b a player, having captured a piece and placed the attacking piece on the captured square, removes his or her hand from the piece;

c in castling, a player's hand has left the rook (once the king has been moved, the castling move must always be completed); or

d in pawn promotion, a player's hand has left the piece that replaces the pawn.

Phases of play Chess players commonly divide a game into three phases: opening game, middle game and end game.

These phases are not clear-cut divisions – they simply reflect the strategies and tactics employed.

1 In the opening game, both players position their pieces into what each considers to be an advantageous situation. Castling moves are usually made during this phase.

2 In the middle game, players attempt to capture enemy pieces, thereby reducing the opponent's attacking ability. However, as the main objective is to checkmate the opponent's king, moves or captures should not be made unless they weaken the opponent's defence of his or her king. The player should also beware of making moves that jeopardise his or her own position.

3 In the end game, players attempt to checkmate the opponent's king. If during this phase a player has few attacking pieces, he or she will attempt – where possible – to promote a pawn into a more powerful piece.

Check and checkmate Whenever a king is attacked by an opposing piece, the king is said to be 'in check'. The check must be met on the following move by either:
a moving the king one square in any direction onto a square that is not attacked;
b capturing the piece that is checking the king; or
c interposing a piece between the king and the attacking piece (if the king is checked by an opponent's knight, it is impossible to intercept the check in this way). A piece that intercepts a check can – in the same move – give check to the opposing king.

Check

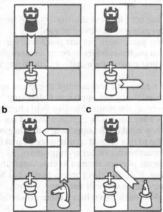

If the checkmate cannot be met then the king is deemed 'in checkmate' or simply 'mate'. When a checking or checkmating move is made, it is customary for the player making such a move to declare 'check' or 'checkmate' as appropriate.

Winning the game

The game is won by the player who:

a checkmates the opponent's king; or

b forces the opponent to resign.

Checkmate may be made, or a player may resign, at any time during the course of the game.

Drawn game

Many games of chess do not end in a victory for either player. A game is drawn in any of the following cases:

a when the player whose turn it is to move can make no legal move (a situation known as 'stalemate');

b when neither player has sufficient pieces remaining on the board to force checkmate;

c when a player can check the opponent's king indefinitely but cannot checkmate it (a situation called 'perpetual check');

d when no capture or pawn move has been made by either participant during 50 successive moves of each player;

e when the same position recurs three times, always when it is the same player's turn to move. In such a case, the right to claim a draw belongs either to the player who is in a position to play a move leading to such repetition (provided that this player declares his or her intention of making this move), or to the player who must reply to a move by which the repeated position is made; or

f when both players agree to call the game a draw.

Illegal positioning

If an illegal move is made during the course of a game, the pieces are set up as they were just before the illegal move. If this is impossible, the game is annulled.

If the pieces are accidentally displaced and cannot be correctly repositioned or if the initial positions of the pieces were incorrect, the game is also annulled.

If the chessboard is found to have been incorrectly placed, the pieces on the board are transferred to a correctly placed board in the same positions as when the error was discovered and play then continues.

CHILDREN'S BAGATELLE

Quite different from the tabletop, adult game of the
same name (see p.64), children's bagatelle is an ancient
precursor to pinball.

Aim

The game requires both skill and luck. Players aim to
shoot the balls onto the board and score the most points.

Equipment

The board is made of wood or plastic. It is rectangular
in shape – approximately 30.5cm x 61cm (1ft x 2ft),
although some are small enough to fit in the hand – and
one of its ends is curved to form a semicircle. Some
boards are illustrated with popular themes.

The board has a raised rim – rather like a tray – and is
slightly sloped so that the far (curved) end is higher
than the end nearest the player. A number of small nails
form semicircles (called 'cups') in the board; other nails
are free standing. There are also a number of shallow
depressions or 'holes' just big enough to hold a ball.
The cups and holes are marked with scoring values,
usually ranging from 5 to 150 points. The free-standing
nails act as deflectors and have no score.

The balls used in bagatelle are small (about 2.5cm [1in]
in diameter) and are made of steel or plastic. When not
in play, they are kept within a special partition running
along the near end of the board. A stick about the size
and weight of a drum stick is used to strike the balls.
On many boards, the balls are released by a spring-
loaded trigger rather than pushed by the player using
the wooden stick. By pulling and releasing the trigger,
the player shoots the balls one at a time so that they are
propelled around the board.

The bagatelle board

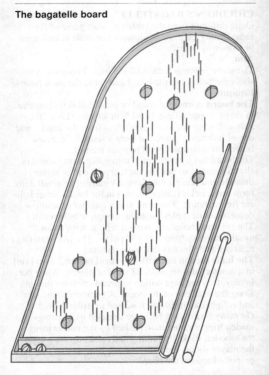

Playing

Any number can play. In turn, each player takes a ball and places it at the head of the channel that runs along the right-hand side of the board. Holding the striking stick with one or both hands, the player then strikes the ball so that it runs along the channel and into the main area of the board.

When shooting, the tip of the stick may not extend beyond the top edge of the channel. If the player strikes the ball with insufficient force – so that it rolls back to the start instead of into the main area of the board – it may be shot again.

If the ball is hit so forcefully that it shoots off the board, however, the player may not take the ball again and the score for that ball is 0.

The number of balls each player may strike in a turn is determined by the players before the start of the game. The players may also decide whether to remove each ball from the board as soon as it has been played, or to leave all the balls in position until the end of a turn.

If balls are removed before the end of a turn, the score must be noted for each ball. If enough balls are available (i.e. the number of balls allowed per turn times the number of players), balls can be left in place until the end of the round. This means that players whose turns come after others may be at a disadvantage if cups or holes are filled by balls of previous players. On the other hand, later players can dislodge the balls of previous players and score points (see **Scoring**).

Scoring

Each player's score is noted after each turn. A ball is not scored or removed until it has come to an absolute standstill. If it comes to a halt inside a cup or hole, it scores the corresponding number of points. There is no score if the ball:

a enters a cup or hole but then rolls out again;

b becomes lodged against the nails outside a cup or hole; or

c comes to a halt in any non-scoring area of the board, including the near end of the board.

If balls are left in position until the end of a round, points may also be scored by a player managing to dislodge an opponent's ball that has already stopped in a cup or hole. For example, if a previous player's ball scored 50 points, a player dislodging this ball may add 50 points to his or her own score – whether or not the ball stopped in the scoring area.

Winning the game

Players may decide to continue a game until:

a a set time limit has been reached;

b one player's score has reached a predetermined number of points; or

c each player has had a predetermined number of turns.

In any case, the player with the highest score is the winner.

DRAUGHTS

Known as checkers in the USA, draughts seems to have
developed from older games in the Middle East. Most
British pubs will have a board and pieces in a box
somewhere, but it is less popular than dominoes, since
draughts is a game for only two players.

Aim

Two players compete to capture all the opponent's
pieces.

Equipment

The board for draughts is made of wood, plastic or
cardboard and is about 36–40cm (14.5–16in) square. Its
surface is divided into 64 squares, eight along each
side. The squares are alternately light and dark
coloured, usually white and black or red and black.
Moves are limited to squares of one colour.

The pieces are wooden or plastic discs about 3.5cm
(1.5in) in diameter. Each player has a set of twelve

Positioning pieces on the board

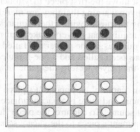

pieces, and the two sets are of different colours –
usually red, white or black.

Starting play

The board is placed between the players so that each
has a light square on the left of the first row. The
players draw lots to determine who plays first; this
player always uses the darker pieces.

The pieces are positioned on the dark squares as shown
in the diagram. (Alternately, if the game is to be played
on light squares, all pieces are first positioned on light
squares.)

Playing

In turn, players each move one piece. All moves must
be diagonal, as pieces can only be moved to an adjacent
dark-coloured square. In addition, all pieces must move
forward only, unless they have been 'crowned' by
reaching the opponent's first row of squares. Crowned
pieces are called 'kings', and they are allowed to move
either backward or forward.

Pieces can only be moved into vacant squares.

Players must move the first piece they touch, unless
they have given warning that they are merely
straightening the pieces within their squares.

Some rules require that players make their moves
within five minutes. If the player has failed to move
after time has been called and a one-minute extension
has passed, the player forfeits the game.

Capturing

A player can 'capture' an opponent's piece if it is in an
adjacent square and there is a vacant adjacent square
beyond that square. To capture, the piece 'leapfrogs'
over the opponent's piece to the vacant square (**a**).

A piece can capture several pieces in one move if possible (**b**). It is not necessary to move in the same

Capturing

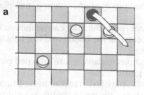

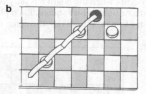

diagonal direction in order to capture several pieces. Captured pieces are removed from the board; they do not come into play again except as the 'crowns' placed on pieces becoming kings.

Players must make capturing moves when possible. If they fail to do so, the opponent points out the error, and the player is forced to make the capturing move.

Crowning

When a piece reaches the opponent's first row of squares, it is crowned, as described previously. A piece that has been removed from the board is placed on top of the crowned piece; after crowning, that player's turn ends.

On subsequent turns, the king can be moved back toward the centre of the board, and can be used to capture pieces.

Non-crowned pieces can capture crowned pieces.

Ending the game

In some games, play lasts until an agreed time limit is reached. In others, the game continues until one player has succeeded in capturing all the opponent's pieces and removing them from the board.

A stalemate occurs when the board has only two kings, each adjacent to a light corner square. Each player has 40 moves to try to win; if both fail, the game is tied.

A stalemate

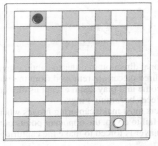

FOX AND GEESE

This developed from a 14th-century Icelandic hunting
game known as hala-tafle. Fox and geese was very
popular in Britain in Victorian inns, where it was
sometimes called wolf and goats.

Aim

Similar games are played in many other parts of the
world. In all of them, two unevenly matched forces
compete against each other. The smaller force usually
comprises only one piece and has considerable freedom
of movement; the larger force is made up of numerous
pieces but has only restricted manoeuvrability.

Equipment

The board Fox and geese can be played on a number
of different layouts. The layout illustrated here
probably gives the two players the most even chance of
winning. Other layouts give the geese an advantage
over the fox. Quite often the board used for nine men's
morris (see p.145) has a fox and geese layout marked
on the other side.

Pieces Any suitable pieces such as checkers, counters,
coins or stones may be used. The one piece
representing the fox must be distinguishable in colour
from the pieces (up to fifteen) representing the geese.

Start of play

The two players decide which of them is to play the fox
and which the geese; they change over after each game.
The pieces are put into position on the board – with the
geese at the top of the board and the fox usually at the
centre (although it may be placed on any vacant point
that the player chooses). Players take alternate turns,
with the fox starting first.

Setting up the board

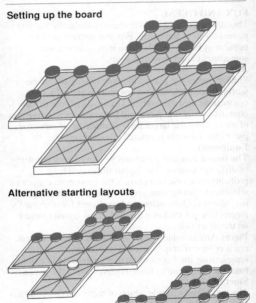

Alternative starting layouts

Playing

The fox may move in any direction along connecting lines, moving one point at each turn (**a**). It may also 'kill' a goose by jumping over it to an adjacent vacant point (**b**); the goose is then removed from the board. The fox may make two or more jumps in one move (killing each goose that it jumps over), provided there is an empty point for it to land on next to each goose that it kills. The fox is obliged to jump if there is no alternate move, even if it puts itself in a vulnerable position by doing so.

Fox's moves

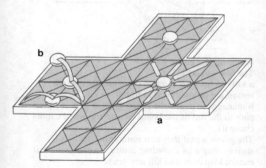

Geese may move along connecting lines in any direction except toward the top of the board (**c**). One goose moves in a turn. Geese may not jump over and capture the fox; their aim is to surround the fox so that it cannot move.

Geese's moves

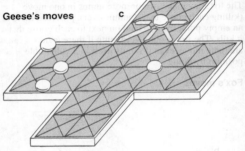

Winning the game

The fox wins if it:

a kills so many geese that there are not enough remaining on the board to trap it; or

b manages to evade the geese so as to give it a clear path to the top of the board (where the geese cannot chase it).

The geese win if they can immobilise the fox by surrounding it or crowding it into a corner, where it cannot leap over and kill any geese.

NINE MEN'S MORRIS

Thought to be one of the world's oldest games, a
version of nine men's morris was probably played by
Stone Age and Bronze Age people. Known by many
other names, especially merrills or merels, this game
appeared in England during the Norman Conquest and
by the 15th century was very popular throughout the
country. Although nine men's morris was played at
many inns, it was also frequently played in churches.
As evidence, morris boards can be found scratched on
pews, floors and windowsills.

Nine men's morris is still played in a few English pubs.
Among them are The Wellington Inn at Darley, near
Harrogate, and The Black Swan at Stratford-on-Avon.
In September the annual World Merrills Championship
is held at Ryedale Folk Museum in the village of
Hutton-le-Hole, North Yorkshire.

Aim

It is a game of strategy for two people in which each
player attempts to capture or block the opponent's
pieces. By placing and manoeuvring pieces on the
board, each player attempts to capture all but two of the
opponent's pieces or to make it impossible for the
opponent to move any piece.

Equipment

The board The game is played on a specially marked-
out board, with three squares, one inside the other, and
with points in the centres of the squares' sides connected
by ruled lines. Bought boards are now usually made of
wood. In the past, they were carved out of stone or even
turf. A satisfactory board can be drawn on paper.

Pieces At the start of the game each player has nine pieces. These may be counters, stones, coins or other appropriate pieces, and each player's pieces must be distinguishable in colour from those of the other's.

The nine men's morris board

Starting play

The players toss a coin to decide which is to start. Each one, in turn, then places one piece on the board at any point of intersection not already occupied by another piece.

Placing the pieces

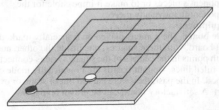

Playing

There are usually three stages of play:

1 placing the pieces on the board;

2 moving the pieces around; and

3 'hopping' them.

The third stage is sometimes disallowed, as it gives one player a distinct advantage over the opponent. Players should decide beforehand whether to allow hopping.

Forming a mill At the beginning, players aim to get three of their own pieces in a straight line along one of the lines of the board, so forming a 'mill'.

A mill

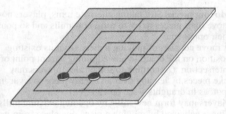

Once a player has formed a mill he or she can 'pound' the opponent by removing one enemy piece from the board. A player may not, however, remove an opponent's piece that is part of a mill, unless there is no other piece available. Once removed from the board, a piece is considered dead for the rest of the game.

Players continue in their turns (nine turns each) until
each of their pieces has been placed onto the board.

Pounding

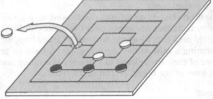

Moving pieces Still taking alternate turns, players now
move their pieces to try to form new mills and so pound
their opponent.

A move consists of moving a piece from its existing
position on the board to any adjoining vacant point of
intersection. (According to some rules, players may
take pieces by leaping over an enemy piece to a vacant
spot, as in draughts – see pp.138–39.)

Players may form new mills by opening existing mills.
This is achieved by moving a piece one place from its
position in a mill, and then returning it at the player's
next move to its original position.

Mills may be broken and re-made any number of times,
and each new mill formation entitles the player to
pound the opponent.

Play continues until one of the players is reduced by
successive poundings to having only two pieces on the
board, or until one player's pieces have been so blocked

by the opponent's pieces that he or she is unable to make any move.

Should a player's only remaining pieces form a mill and it is his or her turn to move, the player must do so even if this results in losing a piece and the game at the opponent's next move.

Hopping is an optional stage of play agreed by the players beforehand. It begins when either player has only three pieces remaining. The player is now no longer restricted to moving pieces along a line to an adjacent point of intersection, but may 'hop' to any vacant spot on the board. This freedom of movement gives the player an advantage over the opponent, restoring the chance of winning.

Winning the game

One player wins the game when:

a the opponent has only two pieces remaining on the board (this is the end of the game when hopping is allowed); or

b the opponent's pieces are blocked by enemy pieces in such a way as to prevent further moves.

SHOVE HA'PENNY

Also known as shove penny or push penny, this game was popular in English inns during Shakespeare's time and remains a widely played pub game throughout the country. It developed from the older and more aristocratic shuffleboard (see p.100), but was illegal until the 18th century.

Its popularity in pubs declined during the 1960s and '70s but it is still played in several pubs in London, including The Blakesley Arms, The Crown and Dolphin and The Kings Arms, all in the East End.

In Stamford, Lincolnshire, weekly league games are played from September to April at pubs such as The Green Man and The Victoria.

The Globe, The Royal Oak and the Red Lion at Swanage, Dorset, are some members of the local league of pubs where games are played on a longer than usual board, known as the Swanage board or Isle of Purbeck shove halfpenny board.

Aim

Two players, or four playing in teams, attempt to position metal discs – or, traditionally, halfpennies – on a marked board. The game is won by the first side to 'shove' three discs into each of the board's nine 'beds'.

Equipment

The board Shove ha'penny is usually played on a special board, but can also be played on any smooth tabletop marked with chalk or pencil. A strip of wood under the board keeps it steady when placed over the edge of a table or other level surface. Boards are 61cm x 35cm (2ft x 1.2ft) and are made of hardwood or slate.

Wood boards have the grain running lengthways, and the sides are marked by shallow grooves.

Ten lines running across the board at 3.1cm (1.25in) intervals mark out the nine 'beds', and two lines at right angles to these beds mark the edges of the scoring area. The squares along the edges of the board are used for recording the players' scores. Some boards have three holes in each square to hold small scoring pegs.

Discs The game was played in Britain long before decimalisation of the currency in 1971. The old halfpenny was 2.5cm (1in) in diameter. Today, players use very highly polished, old halfpennies or similar-sized discs.

The board

Playing
Choice of playing order may be decided by the toss of a coin, or by a preliminary shove for the nine bed (using only one halfpenny except in case of a tie). Each player shoves five discs or halfpennies in turn.

After the preliminary shove, each player's halfpenny or disc is placed partly over the edge of the board and is then shoved as illustrated. A sharp, light tap is most effective. Shoving one halfpenny into another (called 'cannoning' or 'caroming') is an important feature of the game.

The shove

Short shoves Shots that fail to get the halfpenny into one of the beds are called 'short shoves'. They stay in play or are reshot as follows:

a A halfpenny that comes to rest on the nearest line of the first bed must be left in position, but may later be cannoned into the beds by another halfpenny.

b A halfpenny that fails to reach the nearest line of the first bed after hitting a halfpenny on that line must also be left in place.

c A halfpenny that fails to reach the nearest line of the first bed without hitting a halfpenny on that line may be retaken.

A halfpenny is considered dead if:
a it goes wholly beyond the far line of the ninth bed; or
b it stops wholly or partly beyond the side lines in the area used for keeping the score.

Dead halfpennies must be immediately removed from the board and may not be retaken.

Halfpenny on another If a halfpenny stops wholly or partly on top of another, both are left on the board. If a halfpenny remains on top of another at the end of a turn, neither can be scored.

Scoring shots

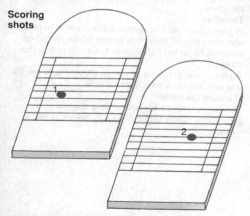

Scoring

A player's turn is scored only after all his or her five
halfpennies have been shoved – hence the importance
of cannoning, which can change a player's score mid-
game. A halfpenny is scored if it lies completely within
one of the beds for which the player needs a score (**1**).
There is no score for a halfpenny on a line (**2**), however
slight the overlap.

Scores may be made in any order, but good players
usually aim to get a halfpenny in the far beds first.

If a player scores more than three times in any bed, the
extra scores may be claimed by the opposition – but not
if this gives the opposition the final score needed to win
the game.

Penalties

A player loses all five shoves for the turn if he or she
touches a played halfpenny before all are played or
removes his or her halfpennies before recording the
score.

A player who plays out of turn is allowed no score for
that turn and must miss the next turn.

Winning the game

The player with the highest score at the end of the
game, after subtracting any penalty points, is the
winner.

SOLITAIRE

Legend has it that a French nobleman who was imprisoned in the Bastille invented solitaire, a game for one person. It is more likely that he, or another originator, adapted the old pub game of fox and geese (see p.141) for play by one person, as the layout of the board for both games is the same.

Equipment

Solitaire can be played on either of two types of board. The original French board is octagonal and has 37 holes for pegs made of wood, ivory, bone or plastic. The later English board is circular, has 33 hollows for glass marbles and a groove running around the outer edge to hold eliminated marbles.

If a traditional board is not available, the positions can be marked on a piece of strong card and small objects such as dice, counters or coins can be used instead of marbles or pegs.

The traditional French board

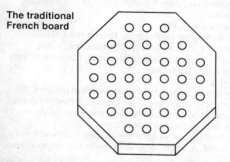

**The traditional
English board**

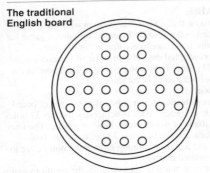

Aim
Some games require all but one piece to be removed
from the board. In others, such as the cross variation
described on p.158, the objective is to make specific
patterns.

Standard solitaire
The starting positions for the French and English
boards are as shown, with all but one hole filled.
Usually, the centre hole is left empty, but some players
choose a different hole.

Playing
Play begins from the centre of the board (or from the
empty hole, if it is not in the centre). A marble (or peg)
'leapfrogs' over a neighbouring marble to fill the empty
hole, leaving its own hole empty.
The marble over which it has jumped is removed from
the board. A single move then leaves two empty spaces.

Starting positions for standard solitaire

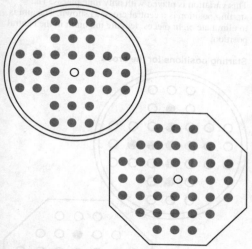

The game proceeds in this manner until only one marble remains in the centre of the board.

Winning a game

A game is completed successfully only if the conditions of play are fulfilled. There may be only one solution, so it is helpful to take note of the moves made. (The solutions for standard solitaire and the cross variation are given on pp.159–61.)

VARIATION: THE CROSS

This variation is played with only nine pieces. The starting position is a central cross, as shown. The aim is to eliminate eight pieces, leaving the ninth in the central position.

Starting positions for the cross

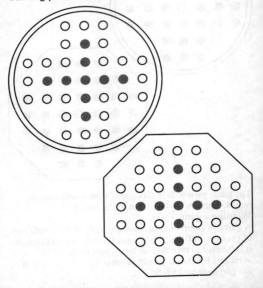

Solutions

The solitaire solutions are described using a system of notation that assigns a number to each hole or place on the board. As a result, moves can be described using two numbers representing the original hole and the hole to which the peg is moved.

Standard solitaire: English board

Read the moves from left to right along each line, using the key to identify the numbers.

5–17 12–10 3–11 18–6 1–3 3–11 30–18 27–25
24–26 13–27 27–25 22–24 31–23 16–28 33–31
31–23 4–16 7–9 10–8 21–7 7–9 24–10 10–8 8–22
22–24 24–26 19–17 16–18 11–25 26–24 29–17

English board hole numbers

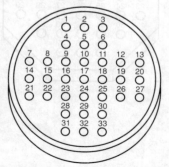

Standard solitaire: French board
Read the moves from left to right along each line, using
the key to identify the numbers.

6–19 4–6 18–5 6–4 9–11 24–10 11–9 26–24

35–25 24–26 27–25 33–31 25–35 29–27 14–28

27–29 19–21 7–20 21–19

French board hole numbers

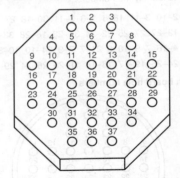

The cross

English board
10–2 24–10 15–17 17–5 19–17 2–10 10–24 29–17

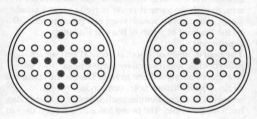

French board
12–2 26–12 17–19 19–6 21–19 2–12 12–26 32–19

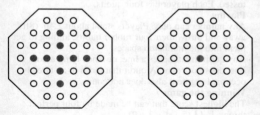

SUFFOLK QUOITS

This old indoor game was played in the county of
Suffolk. Old Suffolk quoits boards may be found in the
attics of a few pubs or in some antique shops in the
area, though the game is rarely played today. A similar
game, called caves, was devised and patented in 1930
by the landlord of a pub in Bury St Edmunds.

Equipment

The board, made of wood, is 46cm (18in) square,
painted white and divided by narrow black lines into
five spaces numbered one to five. The central space is a
circle-shaped shallow hole, surrounded by four
segments of a larger circle, each segment of which also
has a shallow hole. The board has a 2.5cm (1in) strip of
wood stuck under one side so that it slopes toward the
player when it is placed on a table.

The quoits are flat rubber rings, slightly smaller than
the diameter of the shallow holes into which they are
tossed. Each player has four quoits.

Playing

Any number can play. Players stand about 2.4m (8ft)
away and throw their four rubber quoits, aiming to get
them into the numbered spaces.

Any quoit that touches a line, or lands lying across a
line, does not count. A quoit that lands in an already
occupied segment also does not count.

Winning the game

The highest score that can be made by four perfect
throws is 14 (5 + 4 + 3 + 2).

The game ends when one player reaches the exact score
of 21 points. A quoit that takes the score over 21 is
discounted.

VARIATION: CAVES

The board for caves can be square or round, and is usually 30–41cm (12–16in) around. It has five holes about 1cm (0.5in) deep and 9cm (3.5in) in diameter, just a little wider than the diameter of the quoits. The five spaces are numbered with their points value, as in Suffolk quoits.

The quoits are flat rubber rings, as used in Suffolk quoits. Each player has five quoits.

Playing

Players throw their quoits at each turn from a distance of 2.6m (8.5ft), aiming to get them in the shallow numbered holes.

The maximum score for five perfect throws is 15 (5 + 4 + 3 + 2 + 1). Quoits only count if they are fully inside the hole, but two or even three rings can be landed in a hole and be scored.

In caves, play is to 31 up or 61 up.

A caves board with quoits

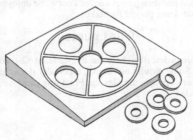

4. Card and dice games

Card and dice games have long been popular pub pastimes. Some card games played in pubs are imports from other countries; others were invented specifically for playing in inns and pubs. Although most reached their peak of popularity as gambling games in the 15th to 17th centuries, and then declined somewhat when legislation restricted gambling in pubs and inns, they have continued to be played as non-gambling games or, where allowed, for small stakes.

Dice games have also been around for centuries, but playing for small stakes is done discreetly, if at all. Although the landlords of pubs in England and Wales have to hold a licence for their customers to play dice games, many are still wary about strangers and may not bring out the game until they are satisfied with a newcomer's credentials.

Betting is against the law in Scottish pubs.

All card and dice games can, of course, be enjoyed without being played for stakes.

Card games

All games described here use the standard 52-card deck. Some require two decks, especially if a large number of people are playing. For a few games, a joker is needed.

ALL FOURS

All fours may have been introduced in Britain in the 17th century, but by the end of the 19th century it had virtually disappeared. Nevertheless, the game is an institution in Blackburn, Lancashire, where it can be found in many pubs as well as in schools and leagues.

Equipment

The standard deck of 52 cards is used with ace ranking high. A set of four cards, one from each player in turn, is called a trick.

Paper and pencil are needed for scoring.

Rank

low   high

Sample tricks

Players

Four people play in partnerships, aiming to score points by 'trumping', and thus winning, tricks.

Dealing

The player with the highest cut becomes dealer. In Blackburn, the rules state that the partnership to correctly guess the colour of the exposed card after the cut plays first. Anyone may shuffle the pack before the cuts are made.

The dealer shuffles the pack. Rotating clockwise and starting from the player on the left, the dealer hands out six cards in packets of three cards face down to each player. The next card is turned face up to assign trumps. The dealer reveals the first trump suit.

By saying 'stand', the player to the left of the dealer accepts the assigned trumps and play begins. The player says 'I beg' if instead he or she wants different trumps assigned.

If the dealer decides to retain trumps, he or she says 'take one' and the player to the left then gains a point and starts play.

If the dealer decides to change trumps, the upcard is put aside, and the dealer hands out a further packet of three cards to each player and turns up the next card to assign the new trumps. If the upcard is the same suit as before, the dealer repeats this process until a new trump is assigned. If the pack runs out, the next player to the left becomes dealer and begins the deal again.

Playing

The player to the left of the dealer places one card face up on the table. Players each follow suit with one card, or they may play a trump card. The trick is taken by the person playing the highest trump or the highest ranking card of the leading suit. The player winning the trick leads for the next trick.

Sample tricks when clubs are trumps

Ace of clubs wins   5 of clubs wins   10 of clubs wins

Untrumped tricks do not score.

Scoring

Tricks are all turned face up at the end of the round. There are 4 points available: 1 each for 'high', 'low', 'jack' and 'game', won by taking tricks containing, respectively, the highest trump, the lowest trump, the J of trumps and the highest number of card points. Card points are as follows:

Ace:	4 points
K:	3 points
Q:	2 points
J:	1 point
10:	10 points

If the J of trumps remains among the undealt cards, only 3 game points are available.

Winning the game

The game is won by the first partnership to reach 11 points. In league play, the match is won by the team to win the most games out of eight.

BRIDGE

Bridge emerged in 1896, a development from the older game of whist (see p.202). Auction bridge evolved in 1904, and in 1925, contract bridge was formulated and soon became the most popular form of bridge. This is the game described here.

Players

Four people play in pairs. Partners sit opposite to each other and are called North–South and East–West respectively.

Equipment

Cards The game calls for the standard deck of 52 cards. Ace ranks high. The 2 is known as 'deuce' and the 3 'trey'.

Rank

high   low

Rank of suits

high   low

A second deck with different backs is often shuffled
while the deal takes place, in preparation for the next
deal.

During the bidding, suits are ranked spades (high),
hearts, diamonds and clubs (low).

Honours are the four aces when there are no trumps.
When there are trumps, honours are the ace, K, Q, J and
10 of trumps.

Bridge score pads and pencils are required.

Scoring pad for contract bridge	We	They

Aim

A partnership aims to win the most points in the best of
three games, known as a 'rubber'.

Preparing

One deck is spread face down, from which each player
draws one card. Those with the two highest cards
become partners, as do the two who draw the two
lowest cards.

The player holding the highest card becomes the dealer
and chooses where to sit, with his or her partner sitting
opposite. If cards of the same value are drawn, they are
ranked by suit.

Any player can shuffle the cards before the dealer

makes the final shuffle and invites the player on the left to cut. Meanwhile, the dealer's partner shuffles the second deck.

Dealing

Beginning with the player on the dealer's left, the cards are dealt singly, face down in clockwise rotation, until each player has 13 cards.

Bidding

When everyone has examined the cards in their hands the auction is begun by the dealer. The other players call in turn in clockwise rotation.

A player can call 'bid', 'pass', 'double' or 'redouble'.

a A pass means a player does not wish to bid; he or she can make another call later. If all four players pass in the first round of the auction, all cards are thrown in and the person to the left of the dealer shuffles and deals again. When three passes follow a bid, double or redouble, the auction ends.

b A player who bids calls the number of tricks in excess of six that his or her partnership will make in a stated trump suit or in no trumps. For example, calls of 'two clubs' or 'five no trumps' means the player believes they can make eight tricks with clubs as trumps, or eleven tricks with no trumps.

Each bid must be higher than the one before it by the player calling a larger number of tricks or a higher ranking trump suit. 'No trumps' ranks highest of all.

The rank order of some sample bids would be:

1 seven no trumps (highest possible call; known as a 'grand slam');

2 six no trumps (known as a 'small slam');

3 five diamonds;

4 four no trumps;

5 four spades;

6 four hearts;

7 four diamonds;

8 four clubs;

9 three clubs; or

10 one clubs (lowest possible call).

c A player who calls double believes he or she could prevent the previous bid from being made if it became the contract. The bid can be outbid by any player as normal, in which case it does not become the contract.

**Sample deal
and bidding**

West leads

South is dealer

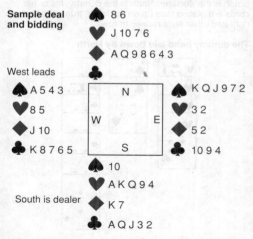

However, if a doubled bid does become the contract, the scores are doubled by the winners if they fulfil their contract or by the partnership that called double if the contract is not fulfilled.

d When their bid has been doubled, one of the bidding partnership may call redouble, reasserting their confidence in their bid. A bid that has been redoubled can be outbid by either partnership.

After bidding
The contract is four hearts to be made by North–South. South is the declarer. North is the dummy; his or her cards are placed face up on the table, trumps to the right and other suits ranked in rows.

The dummy hand laid down by North

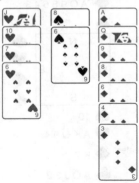

The contract

The partnership from which the highest call came in the auction now has to fulfil that contract during play. Their opponents aim to prevent them.

The declarer

The member of the contracting partnership who first bid no trumps or a trump suit (spades, hearts, diamonds, clubs) is called the declarer and plays both hands. His or her partner, called the 'dummy', lays his or her hand on the table when the lead card has been played, and takes no further part in the play of that deal.

Playing

The first player is the person to the left of the dealer. When the bidding is complete, this player leads by playing any card from his or her hand face up on the table. The trick is completed by each person playing one card in turn, clockwise. The declarer plays a card from his or her own hand and from the dummy hand in correct order.

Every card must follow the leading suit. If unable to follow suit, a player may play a card from another suit.

Winning the trick

a When the contract is a no trump bid, all suits are ranked equally, so the highest card in the leading suit wins the trick.

b When the contract is a bid in trumps, either the highest card in the leading suit or, if any trumps are played, the highest trump card wins the trick.

The winner of one trick leads the next trick.

Some winning tricks

Diamonds lead, no trumps
10 of diamonds wins

Spades lead, clubs trumps
5 of clubs wins

Tricks are piled to show how many have been made. Any trick can be inspected before the inspecting partnership plays in the next trick.

Fulfilling the contract

The contracting partnership is said to have 'made the book' when their first six tricks are taken. They must then make at least the number of tricks they bid. The tricks in the book are piled together so that the extra tricks can be clearly counted.

Scoring

Both partnerships should keep scores to avoid disputes. Scores also affect the strategy of the game. A horizontal line is drawn across the WE (one partnership) and the THEY (the opponents) columns. Points can be scored 'below the line' and 'above the line':

a Below the line (trick points): Only the declarer's partnership scores trick points if they have fufilled the contract for the hand. Only the extra tricks are scored below the line.

b Above the line (premium points): Both sides score premium points if they achieve any of the following in the hand:

1 overtricks (tricks over the number bid);

2 doubling or redoubling successfully;

3 making a slam that was bid;

4 honour cards dealt in the hand;

5 winning the final game of a rubber; or

6 undertricks, which the declarer's partnership fails to make to complete their contract. Their value is added to the opponent's score.

A partnership is said to be vulnerable when its first game towards a rubber has been won. When the score is one game all, both partnerships are vulnerable.

Winning the game

Progress towards winning a game is shown by the number of trick points; 100 or more wins a game. More than one hand may be played.

After each hand, a horizontal line is drawn below the trick scores of both partnerships. Scoring tricks for the next game begins from zero, below this line. Premium scores continue above the line without division.

Winning the rubber

The first side to win two games scores 700 premium points if the opponents have not won a game, 500 if they have. The rubber is won by the partnership with the higher total of combined trick and premium points.

Back scoring

In a competition where partners rotate, the status of an individual is calculated by 'back scoring' after each rubber:

a the losing partnership's score is deducted from the winner's to find the difference;

b the difference is rounded up to the nearest 100 – for example, 750 becomes 800;

c the rounded difference is divided by 100 – for example, 800 becomes 8; and

d the winning partners are given a plus score for the rubber (for example, plus 8). The losers get the same minus score (minus 8).

Winning the competition

As individuals play further rubbers with different partners, they acquire plus or minus scores. At the end of the competition, the player with the highest plus score is the overall winner.

Recording scores on the scoring pad

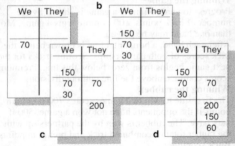

a WE score 70 trick points.

b WE score 30 trick points and 150 premium points. WE win the first game (100 trick points) and a line is drawn across both columns. WE are now vulnerable.

c WE fail to make a contract by two tricks. THEY score 200 vulnerable undertrick points.

d THEY score 60 trick points and 150 premium points.

Scoring table for contract bridge

Declarer's below-the-line trick scores	♣	♦	♥	♠	NT
First extra trick (over six) bid and made	20	20	30	30	40
Subsequent tricks bid and made	20	20	30	30	30
Doubling (double the trick score)					
Redoubling (double the doubled score)					

Above-the-line scores	Not vulnerable	Vulnerable
Small slam	500	750
Grand slam	1000	1500
Undoubled overtrick	Trick value	Trick value
Doubled overtrick	100	200
Redoubled overtrick	200	400
Fulfilling a doubled or redoubled contract	50	50

Rubber, game and partscore	Points
Winning rubber (opponents have no game)	700
Winning rubber (opponents have one game)	500
Winning one game in unfinished rubber	300
Having the only partscore in unfinished rubber	50

Honours (in one hand)	Points
Four trump honours	100
Five trump honours	150
Four aces (no trump contract)	150

Undertricks	a	b	c
First trick (not vulnerable)	50	100	200
Subsequent tricks	50	200	400
First trick (vulnerable)	100	200	400
Subsequent tricks	100	300	600

a = undoubled
b = doubled
c = redoubled

CRAZY EIGHTS

A variation of the games go boom and switch, crazy eights is a simple and sometimes noisy game of pure luck. It can be played by any number of players, and is usually enjoyed by younger groups of pubgoers.

Cards

A standard deck of 52 cards is used in which ace ranks high. The 8s are wild cards.

Aim

Each player, competing against the others, tries to be the first to get rid of all his or her cards.

Dealing

Players cut; highest cut deals seven cards, one at a time, to each player clockwise.

The remaining cards are put face down in the centre of the table.

Playing

All players sort their cards and the person to the dealer's left starts the round by placing one card face up on the table.

The next player, clockwise, adds a card that is:

a the same suit (all hearts etc.); or

b the same rank (number or picture) as the one before.

When a player cannot follow with one of the above, he or she picks cards from the spare pile until drawing a card that can be played.

When the spare pile runs out, a player has to say 'pass' and it is the next player's turn.

The 8s, as wild cards, can be played on any card. The player of an 8 determines which suit must follow.

When everyone has played in that round, the person who played the highest ranking card starts the next round. If there is a tie, the one who played first starts the next round.

Winning the game

The first player to get rid of all his or her cards is the winner. He or she proclaims this by shouting 'boom!', and scores points for all cards still held by other players as follows:

8:	50 points each
K, Q, J:	10 points each
ace:	1 point each
all other cards:	face value

If the spare pile runs out before anyone goes boom, each player counts the value of his or her cards in hand; the winner is the one with the lowest total. The winner then scores the difference between his or her own total and the combined totals of the other players.

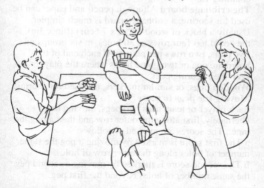

CRIBBAGE

Thought to have been developed by Sir John Suckling, a poet and member of the English court in the early 17th century, cribbage is one of the oldest card games still played. A fast-moving game, it requires a quick mind. It is the only card game which the law allows to be played in pubs for small stakes.

Players

The most popular cribbage played in pubs is the four-handed game for four players, playing in pairs. Partners sit opposite each other. There are variations for other numbers of players as well.

Equipment

Cards A standard 52-card deck is used, all cards having their face value (ace is 1) and court cards counting 10.

The cribbage board Although pencil and paper can be used for scoring, a cribbage board is much simpler. Usually a block of wood 25cm x 7.6cm (10in x 3in), the board has four rows of 30 holes, in six groups of five pairs, two rows per player. At each end of the board are one or two game holes where the players keep their scoring pegs.

Wooden pegs, or similar markers, are used for scoring.

Moving the pegs to score

Each player or team uses two pegs, moving them alternately, first along the outer row and then along the inner. The scores are marked as follows:

a The first score is marked by moving a peg the same number of holes along the outer row of holes.

b The second score is marked by moving a second peg the same number of holes beyond the first peg.

c The third score is marked by using the first peg to count that score beyond the second peg.
d To mark the next score, the peg that is behind is used to mark the score onwards from the front peg.
Scoring in the four-handed game continues until the front peg reaches the game hole by moving up the outer row and back down to the end of the inner row, twice around the board.

Cribbage board

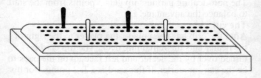

Scoring with pegs

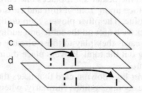

a
b
c
d

Aim

Players try to go twice round the board, getting 121 points.

Dealing

Players cut the deck and the one with the lowest cut is first dealer. The dealer passes the cards to the player on the right for a further cut, then deals five cards, face down and one at a time, to each player. The rest of the deck is put aside.

The crib

Each player then discards one card and places it face down to the right of the dealer to form the crib. The dealer's partnership will claim it as part of its score. The non-dealing partnership gets 3 points from the start to balance the advantage.

The cut

After the crib has been made, the player to the right of the dealer cuts the remaining deck. The top card is turned over by the dealer and left face up on the pack to be the start or starter. If this card is a J, 2 points 'for his heels' are scored by the dealer.

Playing

The player to the dealer's left places one card from his or her hand face up in front of him and calls out its numerical value. The other players then do the same, moving clockwise around the table and adding the value of the cards they play to those already on the table, calling out the total. Players place their cards in front of them.

When a player lays down a card that takes the total to 15, he or she scores 2 points. Similarly, when a total reaches 31 exactly, that player scores 2 points. Other scoring combinations of cards are:

a pair (two cards of the same rank): 2

b pair royal (three of the same rank): 6

c double pair royal (all four cards of the same rank): 12
d run (a sequence of cards in rank order): 1 per card (any suit)
e flush (any four or five cards of the same suit): 1 per card
If also a run, it scores for both a flush and run.
f fifteen (any group of cards with a total face value of 15): 2
Pairs of court cards must match by face – i.e., J pairs with J, Q with Q, etc. Runs do not have to be played in sequential order to count. Flushes are not taken into account during play.

Scoring

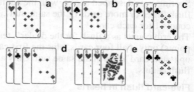

Examples of some calls

If the four players each played a 5, the calls and scoring would be as follows:

Player	Card	Call	Score
player 1	5	'5'	0
player 2	5	'5 for pair'	2
player 3	5	'5 for pair and pair royal'	8
player 4	5	'5 for double pair royal'	12

The first team (players 1 and 3) thus score 8 points, and the second team (players 2 and 4) score 14.

If a player's turn takes the card count over 31, he or she says 'go'. The next player in turn then plays any card low enough to keep the total below 31. If the count then reaches 31 exactly, that player gets 2 points; if it is still less than 31, he or she gets 1 point and calls 'go'. All the cards on the table are turned over and play begins again, but with only the cards remaining in the hands. The game continues until the count reaches 31 or all cards have been played.

The show

When all cards of the hand have been played, the players add up their individual scores.

Scoring is as described above, with the addition of a flush (three or more cards of the same suit), which counts 1 for each card.

The crib counts as a flush for the dealer's team (worth 5 points) only if all four cards, plus the first card turned up ('start card'), are in the same suit. Only a five-card flush counts.

Five-card flush in hearts

start card   cards in hand

Both players can include the start card in their show. For example, if the start card is 4 of hearts and a player has 4 of clubs, 5 of hearts, 6 of clubs and 6 of spades, the scoring combinations of 4, 4, 5, 6, 6 are:

a 8 points for fifteen (four combinations of 4, 5, 6);

b 12 points for runs (four runs of 4, 5, 6); and
c 4 points for pairs (5, 5, and 6, 6),
making a total of 24 points.

Sample show of 24 points

start card   cards from hand

scoring combinations

8 points for fifteen
and 12 points for runs

4 points for pairs

A player holding a J of the same suit as the start card scores 'one for his nob'.

Conventions

A redeal is required if there are errors in dealing. If a dealing mistake is found after play has begun, the non-dealing partnership gains 2 points and the cards are redealt or extra cards are drawn from the stock pile.

If a player does not play the extra cards after a call of 'go', he or she may not play those cards later and the opposing team gains 2 points. There are no penalties for counting errors during play.

Winning the game

The game is played to 121 points. If a pair reaches 121 points before the hand is played out, the game ends immediately.

A team scores an extra game if it reaches a score of 121 before the opponent is halfway round the board – i.e., before the opposing team reaches 61. This is called a 'lurch'.

EUCHRE

This game originated in the Alsace region of France, where it was called jucker, a name which may be the root of the term 'joker' for the extra card incorporated into British decks in the 19th century. It is mostly played in the west of England and in Kent. Most league playing follows the rules of the British Euchre Association, but the size of the stripped deck varies by region. The game described here uses a deck stripped of all cards below the 7, as is played in Exeter and Cornwall.

Players

Four people play in pairs, with partners competing to win tricks.

Cards

Every card below 7 is removed from a standard deck of 52 cards to make a 32-card deck in which ace ranks high, unless the suit is trumps.

In a trump suit the J from the suit of the same colour is included and the ranking order from high to low is J trumps, J suit of same colour, A trumps, K trumps, Q trumps, 10, 9, 8 and 7 trumps.

Rank order when clubs is an ordinary suit

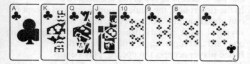

Rank order when clubs is trumps

Preparing

Each partnership takes the 3 and 4 of one suit from the
stripped cards to use as score cards.

The lowest cut of the deck decides who deals. The
dealer shuffles and offers the cut to the player on the
left.

The players should agree at this stage whether they are
going to play for a 5-, 7- or 10-point game.

Dealing

Beginning on the dealer's left, cards are dealt face
down in packets of two cards to each player on the first
round and packets of three on the second round.

The next card, known as the 'upcard', is placed face up
on the table to assign trumps. The remainder are placed
faced down to form a stock.

Bidding for trumps

Starting with the player to the dealer's left, every player
can bid to accept or reject the upcard as trumps.

In the first round, the dealer's opponents can accept by
one player saying 'I order it up', his or her partner by
saying 'I assist' and the dealer can accept by discarding
one card and replacing it with the upcard.

If one player accepts the upcard, play begins.

Alternatively, the upcard can be rejected by non-dealers

saying 'I pass' and by the dealer placing the card face up and visible under the stock.

If all players reject the upcard, a second round of bidding allows each player to either pass or nominate a different suit as trumps. The first nomination becomes the trump suit, and play begins.

If all players pass in the second round, cards are shuffled and redealt by the next player in turn clockwise.

The player who accepted the trump suit in the first round or who nominated it in the second can choose to play solo by declaring 'I play alone'.

This player's partner then places his or her cards face down and takes no further part in that round, although it is still the partnership that scores points.

Playing

The player to the left of the dealer leads with one card face up. Players must then play cards of the same suit. If they cannot follow suit, they play either a trump card or any other suit.

The player of the highest ranking card wins the trick and leads for the next trick.

Scoring

The following points can be gained on a round, sometimes called a 'leg':

a march (all five tricks):	2 points
b march for a solo player:	4 points
c three or four tricks:	1 point
d euchred opponents – i.e., if they have made fewer than three tricks:	2 points

The partners keep their scores by using the two cards from the stripped pack as follows:

a 1 point: place the 3 with the other across it
b 2 points: place the 4 with the other across it
c 3 points: place the 3 on top of the other card
d 4 points: place the 4 on top of the other card

Scoring for higher scores is best done on paper or a cribbage board.

Keeping the scores

  a   **b**   **c**   **d**

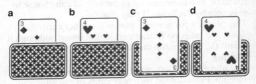

Winning the game

Players agree beforehand how many legs make up a game. The game is then won by the pair winning the most legs.

INDIAN POKER

Considered to be a standard drinking card game as it gets wilder – and some might say more challenging – the more players drink, Indian poker is not for the serious. Any number can play.

Playing

A standard deck of cards is used, from which each player is dealt one card.

Without looking at their cards, each player places his or her card, face out, on their forehead, holding it in place with one finger. The cards must be visible to all the other players.

Players bet on their own cards, basing their evaluation of their cards' worth on the value of the other players' cards.

Players who do not want to bet pass and drop out of the game. As players drop out, the remaining players continue betting until only one is left holding up a card. That player wins.

PONTOON

Also known as vingt-et-un, this is a game of chance for
any number of players. A version of it is played as the
banking game called 21 or blackjack. It can be played
as a gambling game, for small stakes or chips, or as a
non-gambling game.

Cards

A standard deck of 52 cards is needed. If there are more
than seven players, two decks can be used.

The cards have points values as follows: aces count as
11 or 1; court cards count as 10; all others count at face
value.

Individual players may choose to use an ace to count as
11 points or 1 point.

A pontoon

A 'pontoon' consists of two cards that add up to 21.
Any ace with any court card or a 10 makes a pontoon.

Pontoons

The bank

The dealer is chosen by cutting the cards; the player
cutting the highest card deals.

The dealer is also the banker and everyone plays
against the bank.

Everyone then agrees what the maximum stake shall

be. Five chips or small coins, for example, would be a
good starting maximum.

Dealing

The banker shuffles the pack and gives each player –
including him- or herself – one card face down, starting
with the player on the left.

The aim is to collect cards that total 21 points or
approach that, but to avoid going over 21.

Playing

Each player looks at his or her own card, replaces it
face down and places a stake by it in turn. The stake
can be any amount up to the agreed maximum.

Players stake their money (or chips) on getting cards
that total 21.

The banker, however, does not place a stake. If the
banker has a good card, he or she makes a bet by
calling 'double you'.

This means everyone must double the stake already
placed by their cards.

A second card is then dealt face down to each player,
and they inspect both cards.

If anyone, including the banker, has a pontoon – i.e. an
ace and a 10 or a court card – it is revealed and
declared.

Payout on a pontoon

a If it is the banker who has the pontoon, all players
pay twice what each has already staked (or four times,
if the banker has doubled).

b If both the banker and another player have pontoons,
that player only 'pays once', i.e. pays the bank the
original stake (or twice that stake if the bank has
doubled). All other players 'pay twice'.

c If a player, but not the banker, has a pontoon, the banker pays that player twice the stake (or four times, if the bank has doubled).

d If two players have pontoons, and the banker has none, the banker pays them both.

Continuing play

If a pontoon has not been made, the hand continues. Before proceeding, however, some players may want to make splits.

Sample splits

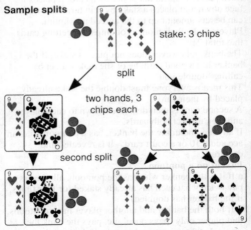

stake: 3 chips

split

two hands, 3 chips each

second split

three hands, 3 chips each

Splits

Anyone who holds two cards of the same rank, such as two 9s or two Js, may split them and have a card dealt on each of them.

If one of the dealt cards is another 9, there could be a further split.

A split must be declared. It is then played as two (or three) separate hands, each carrying the original stake (doubled if the bank has doubled).

Two or more players who want to split in the same round can do so in turn.

If a pontoon is made it must be declared as before.

Play continued: stick, twist or buy

Players now have the option of how their next card is dealt.

The banker begins with the player to the left and asks if players want to 'stick', 'twist' or 'buy'.

If a player's cards add up to 21 or almost 21, the player calls 'stick' (to take no further cards), and the next player takes a turn. Players can only declare 'stick' if the points count of their cards is 16 or more. If the count is 15 or less, players must twist or buy.

'Twist' means a card dealt face up.

'Buy' means a card dealt face down but the player must increase the stake. The amount must not be more than double what is already staked.

If a player buys for an extra stake of, say, two chips, no more than two chips can be staked for any further buys.

A player who has twisted is not allowed to buy on that hand, but may twist on two further turns only.

A player who has bought has the choice of twist or buy again, under the same conditions as before.

Some hands

20 points: stick   25 points: burst   24 points: burst

17 points: stick   19 points: stick

20 points: stick   18 points: stick

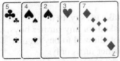

21 points: stick

Five-card, non-bursting hands pay double stakes.

Burst

If a player is dealt a card that takes the total for the hand above 21, the player calls 'burst', throws the cards face up on the table and pays the stake to the bank, taking no further part.

The payout

When everyone has had a turn, the banker puts his or her cards face up on the table and buys or twists cards until either sticking or bursting.

If the banker bursts, each remaining player is paid an amount equal to the player's stake.

If the banker sticks, the remaining players compare the points value of their cards with the banker's. The banker then pays the amount of their stakes to those whose hand has a higher points value than the bank's. Players whose points value is equal to or less than the bank's pay their stakes to the banker.

The five-card trick

The maximum cards a player may collect is five.

Any player who collects five cards without bursting is paid double the stake by the bank, regardless of the points value of the cards.

Limitation on buying

A player may buy three cards to make up a five-card trick. However, if the fourth card gives the player a points total of 11 or less, the player is obliged to twist for the fifth card, because it is certain to make 21 or less. A player is not allowed to bet on a certainty.

Changing the bank

A player who gets a pontoon usually takes over the bank after the deal has been completed, and then shuffles the cards and makes a new deal. There are

three conditions under which the deal remains with the
same banker:
a when a pontoon is declared in the first round of a new
bank;
b when there are two or more pontoons in the same
round; or
c when a pontoon has been built on only one of a pair
of split cards.

The joker variation

Some players like to include the joker in the pack,
which is wild, i.e. it can stand for any card the player
chooses.

RUMMY

Internationally one of the most popular card games, rummy evolved from rum poker, which was played in 19th-century saloons in the USA. This is the basic rummy game; a wealth of variations are possible using these rules as the foundation.

Players

Any number from two to six can play, each person playing for him- or herself. The aim is to be the first to go out by melding all one's cards.

Cards

The standard deck of 52 cards is used and ace ranks low. J, Q and K of each suit are worth 10 points each; all other cards are face value, with ace worth 1 point. Melds are made by:

a grouping three or four cards of the same rank; or
b making a sequence of three or more cards of the same suit.

Melds

group   sequence

Preparing

The first dealer is chosen by low cut. He or she then shuffles the cards and invites the player on the right to cut the pack. A winning score is agreed and scores are kept on paper.

Dealing

Cards are dealt singly in clockwise rotation, the number depending on how many players there are:

a two players are each dealt ten cards;
b three to four players are each dealt seven cards;
c five to six players are each dealt six cards.

A deal when there are six players

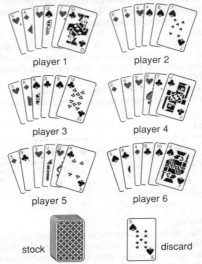

player 1

player 2

player 3

player 4

player 5

player 6

stock

discard

A stock is made by turning the pile of undealt cards face down. A discard pile is begun by turning up the top card from the stock and placing this upcard on the table, next to the stock.

Playing

The player to the left of the dealer begins by choosing to take either the upcard or the top card from the stock. He or she may then lay face up on the table any meld in hand. Finally, a card must be discarded. This can be any card except the one taken from the discard pile. Play proceeds clockwise. After laying down melds, players may additionally lay off extra cards on melds already formed by other players.

The round ends when a player goes out – i.e. uses all his or her cards, with or without a final discard. A player goes rummy when going out all in one hand without any previous melding or laying off of cards. If no player has gone out before the stock is used up, a new stock is made by turning the discard pile face down, without shuffling.

After a player has gone out, there is a new deal for the next round. The deal passes clockwise from the first dealer.

Scoring

When a player goes out, his or her score is the combined numerical value of all the opponents' cards in hand. When a player goes rummy, the score is doubled.

Winning the game

The first player to reach the agreed score wins the match.

WHIST

Whist became popular when Edmond Hoyle described it in the first published rule book of card games in 1746. It was a refinement of the older game of triumph, sometimes called whisk. Whist has since spawned many challenging games such as solo whist and contract bridge.

Players

Four people play in pairs. Partners sit opposite each other and cooperate to win tricks.

Cards

The standard deck of 52 is used. Ace ranks high.

Dealing

The first dealer is chosen by high cut for which ace ranks low. Any player can shuffle the cards before the dealer makes the final shuffle and invites the player on the right to cut the pack.

The whole pack is dealt in clockwise direction. Cards are dealt singly, face down, except the last one which is turned up to assign trumps for that hand. The dealer claims this card when making his or her first play.

There is a misdeal if any player receives fewer or more than 13 cards or if any but the last card is revealed. Players can agree to proceed after mistakes are corrected, or to have a redeal before the first trick. The redeal passes to the next player clockwise.

Playing

The first player to the left of the dealer leads the play by laying a card face up in the middle of the table. Each person in turn plays one card of the leading suit face up. Anyone who cannot follow suit may use a trump or any other card.

The trick is won by the person playing:
a the highest trump card; or
b the highest ranking card of the leading suit.

Sample tricks

leading suit clubs:
ace of clubs takes the
trick

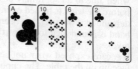

8 of clubs takes the trick

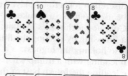

leading suit hearts,
diamonds trumps:
2 of diamonds takes the
trick

The winner claims the trick by turning it face down in front of him or her, and leads play for the next trick.
The game continues until the hand of 13 tricks has been completed.
If all 13 tricks are won by one partnership, it is called a 'slam'.

Subsequent deals for each new hand pass clockwise to the next player, who shuffles as before. A new trump suit is declared at each deal.

Conventions

a A revoke is caused by not playing the leading suit when able to do so. It may be corrected without penalty before the trick is turned over. Penalty points can be demanded if the trick has been turned over. The whole hand is abandoned for a new deal if both partnerships revoke.

b A card exposed when not being played must be left face up on the table. The opposition then call at their discretion for it to be played during the hand. It may not be used to make a revoke.

Common techniques include:

a finessing by playing the third highest of a suit when also holding the highest;

b leading with a trump when holding five or more;

c leading the fourth best of the longest suit;

d showing that ace is held by leading K; and

e playing low as second player and high as third player.

Scoring game points

Game points can be won from tricks, honour cards and penalties. Partnerships keep a record of the number of tricks made in each hand. The first six tricks do not score. Tricks seven to thirteen score 1 game point each – for example:

| tricks in each hand: | 6 7 2 10 8 4 etc. |
| game points from hand: | 0 1 0 4 2 0 |

From this stage onwards scoring systems differ, depending on whether the game is the 7-point version or the 5-point version, described here.

The 5-point game is used in English whist. In addition to points from the seventh trick upwards, there are points from honours, revokes and winning games.

a Four points are gained by partnerships holding all four honour cards, which are ace, K, Q and J of trumps. In addition, 2 points are gained by holding any three honour cards.

Trick points take precedence over honour points if both partnerships reach a score of 5 points in the same deal. At the end of the game, the losers' honour points, if any, are discounted.

b Revokes attract 3 penalty points, allotted according to one of the following alternative rulings which must be agreed for the whole match:

1 3 points are lost by the revoking couple;

2 3 points are gained by their opposition; or

3 3 points are transferred from the revokers to the opposition.

c A game is declared when a partnership gains 5 points. The hand may be played out for additional points. The winners of the game get 3 extra points if opponents have a nil score; two if opponents have 1 or 2 points; and one if opponents have 3 or 4 points.

Winning the match

Three games make a match, called a 'rubber'. If the first two games are won by the same partnership, the third game is not played. The partnership winning two games gets 2 extra points towards their final score. The match is won by the partnership with the highest points total at the end of a rubber.

Dice games

Games using dice have been played in English inns for at least 500 years and have always been popular among seafarers.

Dice are available in some pubs in the Channel Islands and along the south coast of England.

Since dice are usually used to gamble for small stakes, some landlords hold licences that allow dice games, while others keep their dice sets hidden and hand them only to known customers. As gambling is illegal in Scotland's pubs, dice will not be found there. Here are described ways of passing a happy hour playing dice with little or no gambling involved.

Dice

A standard modern die is a regular cube, with the six sides numbered with dots from 1 through 6.

Any two opposing sides add up to 7.

Odds

With one true die, each face has an equal chance of landing face up. With two dice thrown together, some scores are more likely than others because there are more ways in which they can be made.

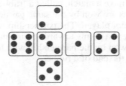

CHICAGO

Chicago, also called rotation, is a game for any number of players. Two standard dice are used. The game is based on the 11 possible totals of the two dice – 2, 3, 4, 5, 6, 7, 8, 9, 10, 11 and 12 – and so consists of 11 rounds. The aim is to score each of these totals in turn.

All dice combinations in sequence

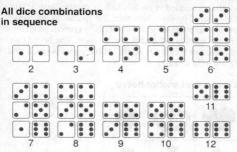

2   3   4   5   6

7   8   9   10   11   12

Playing

Each player in turn rolls the dice once in each round. During the first round, each player tries to make a total of 2; during the second, a total of 3, and so on up to 12. Each time a player is successful, that number of points is added to his or her score. For example, if the player is shooting for 5 and throws a total of 5, he or she gains 5 points.

Failing to make the desired number means the player scores nothing on that throw.

Winning the game

The player with the highest score is the winner.

CROWN AND ANCHOR

This is a simple betting game played among sailors in the Navy. It spread to fishing and merchant fleets, and in World War I was popular in the Army. The game is available in many pubs but usually only on request.

Equipment

All that is needed is an oil cloth or plastic 'board' and three dice. The dice, however, are special to the game and all have the same six symbols: a crown, an anchor, a heart, a diamond, a club and a spade. The board can be folded or rolled up, so the whole game is small and lightweight to carry.

A crown and anchor board

**The six sides of a
crown and anchor die**

Playing

Any number of players can participate, each being the banker in turn. The first banker is chosen by agreement or by the toss of a coin.

Each player places his or her bets on the board. Any amount can be staked on any of the six squares. Chips or other markers can be used instead of money.

The banker then rolls all three dice together. The banker pays out on bets that are on the three squares that match the three dice.

The payout

The amount of the payout varies if two or more dice turn up the same square, as follows:

a on a symbol that turns up on only one die, the banker pays evens, i.e. matches what the player staked;

b on a symbol that turns up on two dice, the banker pays 2 to 1, i.e. double the player's stake; and

c on a symbol that turns up on all three dice, the banker pays 3 to 1, i.e. three times the player's stake.

The banker takes from the board all the stakes that have not won.

The next player then takes a turn as banker. Since the odds are in favour of the banker, rotation gives everyone an equal chance. The game can run for as many rounds as players agree, but to be fair it should only end when everyone has been banker for the same number of turns.

DROP DEAD

This is an exciting game for any number of players using five dice. The aim is to make the highest total score.

Playing

In turn each player begins by rolling the five dice. Each time the player makes a throw containing a 2 or a 5, he or she scores nothing for that throw, and any die or dice that showed a 2 or a 5 must be excluded from any further throws made on that turn. A player's turn continues until his or her last remaining die shows a 2 or a 5 – at which point the player 'drops dead' and play passes to the next player.

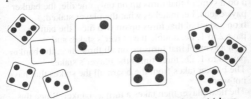

Player rolls a 2 or 5 on the last die and must 'drop dead'

Scores are recorded at the end of each player's turn, and the winner of the game is the player with the highest score at the end of an agreed number of rounds.

FIFTY

This fast-moving game, for two or more players, is one
of the simplest dice games. It requires only two
standard dice.

Playing

Each player in turn rolls the two dice, but scores only
when identical numbers are thrown (two 1s, two 2s and
so on). All these doubles, except two 6s and two 3s,
score 5 points. A double 6 scores 25 points; and a
double 3 wipes out the player's total score, taking him
or her back to 0.

Scoring doubles

5 points | 25 points | wipe out:
return to 0

Winning

Players record their scores on paper after each turn.
They continue rolling in turn until one player reaches
50 points and wins the game.

POKER DICE

Like the card game of the same name, poker dice combines skill and chance. It requires a special set of five dice, each marked with ace, king, queen, jack, 10 or 9 on its six faces.

Set of poker dice

Playing

The first player tosses the five dice together. Aiming to build up the best poker hand, the player can choose to make second and third tosses. On these tosses, he or she can roll all five dice or leave some as they landed. Hands are scored as follows (in order, low to high):

1 highest single die
  (ace is high)

2 pair

3 three of a kind

4 sequence

5 full house (pair plus three of a kind)

6 four of a kind

7 five of a kind

Once the first player's turn has ended and his or her hand is recorded, the next player clockwise takes a turn. Subsequent players can only make as many tosses as the first player made – e.g. if the first player chose to roll only once, all other players can roll only once.

Winning the game

The player with the highest hand wins the game. If two hands tie, the one with higher ranking cards wins.

ROUND THE CLOCK

This is a game for three or four players, using two standard dice. The aim is to throw the dice so they equal 1 through 12 in correct sequence.

Playing

Players throw both dice at once on each turn.

From 1 through 6, a player can score with either one of the two dice or with both of them – e.g. a throw of 3 and 1 can be counted as 3, 1 or 4. It is also possible at this stage to score twice on one throw – e.g. if a player needs 2 and throws a 2 and a 3, both of these numbers can count in sequence.

From 7 through 12, however, a player will obviously always need the combined spot values of both dice to score.

Sample rolls

roll of 5 and 1 can count as:
6 or 5 and 1

roll of 3 and 4 can count as:
7 or 3 and 4

Winning

The winner is the first to complete the sequence.

SHUT THE BOX

A game for two or more players, shut the box may have developed in Europe, though its origins remain a mystery. In this country, it was first played only in the south. Now, however, it is played in pubs throughout Britain, including The King's Arms at Christchurch, Hampshire, and The Harbour Lights Hotel on Alderney. Any number can play.

Equipment

Dice Two standard dice are used in shut the box. A dice cup is used to throw them.

The box The game is played on a lined board, with low tray-like sides, in which there is a row of small boxes numbered 1 to 9. Each box has a sliding lid, all of which are open at the beginning of the game. If a traditional box is not available, a board can be improvised by marking nine numbered boxes on a sheet of card or heavy paper and using coins or counters to 'cover' the 'boxes' during play.

A traditional box

Aim

Players try to cover as many of the numbers as
possible, in accordance with the throws of the dice.

Playing

The player taking first turn throws the two dice onto the
playing tray. The total number rolled can be used to
close any combination of boxes adding up to that total.
For example, a throw of 10 (such as 5 and 5) would
allow the player to cover boxes 6 and 4; 7 and 3; 8 and
2; 9 and 1; 4, 5 and 1, etc.

The same player then throws the two dice again and
tries to cover another two boxes. Players are not
allowed to use combinations involving numbers that
they have already covered.

After covering boxes 9, 8 and 7 a player may throw
only one die on a turn.

A player's turn continues until he or she is unable to
make use of a combination from the latest throw. All
the uncovered numbers are then added up to determine
the penalty score.

All boxes are then re-opened, and play then passes to
the next player.

Winning

A round is finished when all players have had a turn.
The winner is the player with the lowest penalty score
from uncovered boxes at the end of the round.

5. Miscellaneous games

There are many pub games, both traditional and quite
new, that do not fit easily into the usual games
categories. Here are described a few of these oddballs.
They range from animal games, past and present, to
variations of skittles using humans as targets.

Animal racing

It is no secret that illegal contests were commonplace in
yards and fields behind inns in years gone by. Such
cruel activities as cockfights, dog fights and badger
baiting, all to the death, are now rare, fortunately; their
legacy only lives on in such colourful inn names as The
Fighting Cocks and The Dog and Duck.

However, the racing of animals whose reward is food
and freedom may be regarded with some tolerance,
since the animal usually has its own way and moves at
its own speed.

Races in pubs between small animals are sporadic
events and may be casual or organised. In either case,
the purpose of racing is to lay bets on the performance
of your creature. Proceeds usually go to a local charity.

TORTOISES

The Times ran a story in 1938 in which a certain Rev. R.
Allport of Weymouth, Dorset, expressed his
disapproval of tortoise racing, which had become
popular in the county. Apparently the tortoises were
pets from home who raced on the billiards table in the
taproom.

MICE

The *Daily Mirror* reported on a mouse race that turned out to be a disaster for the landlord, held at a pub in Bishops Aukland, Durham, in the early 1970s.

The mouse race was to be held on Derby Day. A track 2.4m (8ft) long had been constructed with lanes for eighteen runners. The mice would be let loose at one end and, in theory, run towards the cheese awaiting them at the other. The first mouse to get the cheese would be the winner.

On the day, the mice were put on the track, but nothing much happened and none of the mice seemed at all interested in running for the cheese.

It turned out that all eighteen mice had been kept together for a week before the race. Consequently fifteen of them were pregnant and, it is said, the other three were so tired out all they wanted was to sleep!

FERRETS

The Queen's Head at Eye in Suffolk holds the annual
Ferret Racing Championships (of the world) every
September.

People come from far and wide. The ferrets are all bred
and tamed in Britain; many of them are personal pets.
During the contest, each ferret is timed as it runs down
a 9m (30ft) length of drainpipe. The record is said to be
fifteen seconds.

INSECTS

A pub in Evesham was once renowned for its well-organised beetle races, and it is said that a farmer introduced woodlouse racing at The Mount pub in Stanton, Gloucestershire.

Beetle racing was popular during both world wars among soldiers in the trenches. One description of a beetle race has all the starters captured under an empty upturned jam jar or tin. A circle is marked about 1m (1yd) around the edge of the jar. At a given signal, the jar is lifted and the owner of the beetle to be first across the line of the circle collects all the bets.

In pub races, there is an entrance fee per beetle and generally six beetles race on a specially constructed race track over a distance of about 1m (1yd).

At Evesham, the beetle speed record over that distance is said to be two seconds.

MAGGOTS

It is said that maggot racing was revived in a Yorkshire pub in 1989. And it has been reported that in 1991 The Farrier's Arms at Grasscroft near Oldham, just across the county border in Lancashire, held its first maggot race to raise money for charity.

Customers had to bring their own champion maggots in matchboxes. The maggot was placed into the sleeve of the matchbox, up against a cardboard gate at one end of a ten-lane race track.

The track was 30cm (12in) long and specially made with artificial grass.

When the cardboard gate was lifted, the race started. A bright light was shone on the maggots from behind, the theory being that they would chase their own shadows.

Owners and onlookers alike were required to sponsor a maggot for £2. The owner of the winning maggot got a bottle of wine while the rest of the money went to charity.

The great joy of such races is that the creature moves so slowly, there is no knowing which, if any, will win. Furthermore, maggots and other small creatures have a tendency to curl up and go to sleep or wander off the tracks in search of a mate, all such activities adding to the excitement of the race. Anyone treating a maggot badly would be disqualified and fined.

Eccentric games

Strange versions of skittles appear from time to time at pubs where the regulars are eager to persuade visitors to take part in these bizarre events. Other games involve people bashing each other with the weirdest of objects.

CONGER CUDDLING

In this game the skittles are human. Dressed in an odd assortment of clothing, the human skittles stand on large upturned flower pots.

The missile with which players attempt to knock the skittles off their perches is a 1.5m (5ft) long conger eel (dead), hung from a rope.

If an eel isn't available, it is said that any other large dead fish will do.

One team acts as the skittles while players on the other team, in turn, attempt to dislodge them from their plant pots by swinging the eel at them. Each player has an agreed, limited number of swings.

Points are scored for every skittle knocked off his or her plant pot or forced to leave it.

Teams change places for the second round. The number of rounds is agreed in advance and the winners are the team with the highest points score at the end of the match.

VARIATION: MARROW DANGLING

This is a variation of human skittles played at The Greyhound pub in Wargrave, Berkshire. In this game, the human skittles also stand on upturned plant pots but protect their heads by wearing plastic buckets with eye-holes made in them.

The opposing team has to try to knock the buckets off by swinging an over-ripe marrow, which is attached to a rope, at the players.

The aim is to gain points by knocking buckets off heads, although bonus points can be earned by knocking the skittle off his or her perch at the same time. A skittle that falls with the bucket intact is a no-score.

DWYLE FLUNKING

The origins of this game, an exercise in lunacy, are unknown. Whether ancient or relatively recent, however, it is surprisingly popular in several English pubs, including the Farmer's Boy in Kensworth, Bedfordshire, where it is played two Sundays a month.

Equipment

The materials needed for dwyle flunking are easily improvised. The 'dwyle' is a beer-soaked rag, about 22cm by 30cm (9in by 12in). It is impaled onto the end of a broom handle, called the 'swadger', which is held by the pitching player.

Players dress up in odd costumes of whatever 'rustic' clothing is available.

A bucket of beer (preferably stale) is available for repeated dunkings of the dwyle. (In some regions a player making a completely missed pitch is required to drink the beer as a penalty.)

Some rules require that players use a length of string to tie their legs together below the knees, and that an accordion be played to signal the dancing time leading up to a pitch, as in musical chairs.

Players

The game is played between two opposing teams of twelve players each. Each player on a team makes one pitch, called a 'flunk', in turn. An inning is completed when both teams have pitched.

Playing

The team not pitching stands in a circle, joining hands. One player from the other team stands in the middle of the circle, holding the swadger on which the dwyle is impaled. Beside the player is the bucket of beer.

The accordionist begins to play, signalling the start of the turn. The players in a circle then dance around the central player, moving clockwise; the central player, meanwhile, moves around the circle in a counter-clockwise direction.

When the music stops, it is time for the flunk. The central player tosses the dwyle toward any opposing player, aiming to make a hit.

Scoring

If a player is hit on the face, the pitching team wins 3 points. A hit on the torso is worth 2 points, and one on a leg or arm is worth 1.

Winning the game

The teams play two complete innings, after which the scores are totalled. The team with the higher score wins.

HAXEY HOOD

An old ceremonial game, originally played between villages, Haxey hood is a rough romp akin to 18th-century versions of football. The game can last until late into the night, and is easily adapted to any location. To date it is still played between three or four pubs in and near Haxey, where the county boundaries of Yorkshire, Nottinghamshire and Lincolnshire meet.

The annual ritual

On 6th January – unless it is a Sunday, when it takes place on the 5th – the King of the Boggans with twelve Boggans and a Fool appear on the Church Green at the Isle of Axholme.

King Boggan wears riding breeches, boots and a long red hunting coat. His hat is decorated with artificial flowers and he holds a walking staff which has a tuft on top and is wrapped in willow twigs. He is from the pub who won the Haxey hood the previous year.

The Boggans wear red jumpers and old trousers or jeans. People taking the part of the Boggans are experienced players, an equal number from each of the participating pubs.

The Fool wears bright, patched trousers, a red jumper, jacket or t-shirt and a green skull cap. The cap is decorated with badges and feathers.

The hood

The real hood is a ball of rope enclosed in a leather bag. However, twelve lesser hoods of rolled-up sacking are used for the first games. The final, thirteenth, game is played with the leather hood.

The pub teams

Each participating pub has a team of an agreed number

of apprentices who wear anything old and are cheered on by their supporters.

The start of the ceremony

The Fool stands on a mounting block near the church and makes a traditional speech explaining the rules of the game. The speech ends with the words:

'Hoose agen hoose, toune agen toune. If thou meets a man hook 'im down. But don't hurt him.'

As the Fool speaks these final words, the Boggans light some damp straw at the base of the mounting block, to 'smoke the Fool out'.

Throwing the hood

After the opening ceremony, King Boggan leads the way to the top of nearby Haxey Hill, where he stands, holding the first hood, at the centre of a circle of Boggans. The circle has a radius of about 46m (50yd). The apprentices stand outside the circle until the King Boggan throws the hood into the air.

Capturing the hoods

Once the hood is in the air, the apprentices try to capture it and carry it off to any of the participating pubs. The Boggans are the guardians of the hood and try to prevent its loss. Hence the need for some practical rules!

Once the hood is inside the door of one of the pubs, the apprentice who placed it there is rewarded with a small sum of money. It does not matter which pub it is taken to; the individual apprentice gets the reward.

Everyone returns to the hill. The King Boggan then throws the second hood as before and the scramble by apprentices to capture it is repeated. The process is then repeated for the remaining eleven lesser hoods.

The final hood

When the King Boggan throws the final, leather hood into the air, everyone joins in – apprentices, Boggans, other regulars from each pub.

The aim is to capture the hood and get it back to your home pub. The scrum that ensues is known as the 'sway' and continues until someone gets the hood over the threshold of his or her home pub.

The winning pub keeps the hood hung behind the bar until the next year.

RHUBARB THRASHING

This is an old game played by two contestants who are blindfolded and have their ears plugged. They each stand inside a large plastic bag inside a dustbin.

Holding each other by the left hand they thrash each other with a stick of rhubarb held in the right hand. The winner is the one to remain inside his or her bin the longest.

PASSING THE SPLOD

The splod in this game is one of those rubber suction pads on the end of a short handle, used to unblock the waste pipe in a sink. The splod is removed from the stick before playing.

This is a contest between two teams who play at the same time. Each team needs one splod and a bucket of water. Players are shirtless or wear t-shirts rolled up to expose the stomach.

The teams stand in line with the first players at one end, each holding their team splod, with a bucket of water nearby. The referee stands at the other end of the lines. At a signal from the referee, the first player dips the splod into the water, then slaps it onto the naked stomach of his or her nearest teammate, shouting the traditional cry of 'splod off!'

The teammate then pulls the splod off his or her own stomach and repeats the whole performance, sticking the splod onto the next player in the line. A splod that falls off must be replaced.

The team that is first to get their splod onto the stomach of the last teammate in line is the winner.

Games of chance

BINGO

A modern development of the old game of lotto, bingo
is played for prizes. In Britain, many cinemas were
converted into bingo halls, but some larger urban pubs
run their own regular bingo and lotto sessions, usually
for a local charity.

Equipment

Bingo cards vary according to the game. In Britain,
two types of bingo are played. 'Prize' bingo – usually
played at fairgrounds or at non-commercial sessions –
is played for prizes other than cash, using a card which
is divided into five rows of five squares each and has
the letters B, I, N, G and O printed at the top of the
card, one letter relating to each column. Numbers
selected from 1 to 75 fill all the squares, except the
central one – a free play square – which is blank and
can be used to complete a central row or column.

At commercial bingo sessions, cards are sometimes pasted on a piece of cardboard called a 'lapboard' – this forms a convenient table and ensures that players do not take their cards home at the end of the session.

Cardboard or plastic markers may be used to cover the numbers, and sometimes cards have sides that can be finger-tipped across the numbers.

Bingo balls are numbered 1 to 99, like the cards.

Machines to mix and select the numbers, usually partly or fully automatic, may be either wire mesh cages or glass or plastic 'blower' machines. The balls are released from the machines one at a time.

Many establishments have a master board connected to a lighted signal board; this diplays the numbers as they are placed on the master board and can also be used to check previously called numbers.

Playing

At the start of each round of calling, the players buy one or more cards. Often they hope to increase their chances of success by buying as many as ten or more cards. As each ball emerges from the selector machine, the caller announces its number and places it on the master board. Any player whose card shows the drawn number covers the appropriate square or squares. (The same number may appear on more than one card, although no two cards are exactly alike.)

Winning

The first player to complete a line of numbers – vertically, horizontally or diagonally – calls 'bingo!' The winner's card is then read back aloud to the caller by a floor attendant, and if it tallies with the master board the player gets a prize.

A single winning line, however, rarely brings in the big money! Most players have their sights set on the jackpot. This is won by the first player to achieve a 'blackout' or 'coverall' (i.e. covering all the numbers on the card). Some bingo halls place a limit on the amount of the jackpot; others let it accumulate from week to week until it is won.

Other winning variations include:

a covering the eight numbers around the central free play square;

b covering the numbers at the four corners of the card; and

c covering specific lines, or lines that intersect to form a stated letter of the alphabet.

When a game has been won, any player may keep or exchange his or her card(s) for a further game or buy additional cards, but the selection of numbers starts afresh.

LOTTO

This family game – the forerunner of bingo – originated in Italy and has been played in England for more than a century. Other names by which it is known are housey housey, tombola and bolito.

Equipment

Lotto is played with special rectangular cards divided into either three or five horizontal rows and nine vertical columns.

Each horizontal row has five numbered squares and four blank squares. The arrangement of the numbers is random, except that the vertical columns contain, from left to right respectively, numbers from 1 to 10, 11 to 20, 21 to 30, and so on up to 90. No two cards are alike.

Complementary to the cards is a set of 90 small card counters numbered from 1 to 90, and a sufficient number of markers.

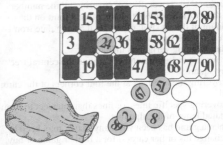

Playing

As many players may take part as there are cards. Each player is given one card – or more than one if there are any left over.

One player (who may also take part in the game if desired) is the caller. He or she puts the card counters into a sack or other container and mixes them well. The caller takes out one counter at a time and calls its number. The player or players with a card on which the number appears places a marker on the appropriate square.

Winning the game

A player who has covered all of the numbers on his or her card calls out 'lotto!' The card and counters are checked, and if they match correctly that player wins the game.

SPINNING GAMES OF CHANCE

Spinning Jenny, twister, wheels, Norfolk wheel and put-and-take are regional names for gambling games involving a primitive roulette wheel. In Manchester and Salford, pubs traditionally used the small teetotum, which was a cardboard toy spinning top.

Some elderly customers in East Anglian and Kentish pubs remember spinning games being played for large stakes on market days.

VARIATION: PUT-AND-TAKE

In the 1920s and '30s this game was the focus of a big gambling craze, both in Britain and in the USA, but the use of 'loaded tops' and rampant cheating meant it soon died out. Now, however, the game seems to be coming back into fashion. It can be played by any number of players.

An eight-sided top, sometimes made of cardboard, is used, with sides marked 'put 1', 'take 1', 'put 3', 'take 3', 'put 4', 'take 4', 'put-all', and 'take-all'. (In some regions, including the Midlands, a five-sided top is sometimes used.)

Each player contributes an agreed amount to the pot. Players then take turns to spin the top.

If the top lands with a 'put' side uppermost, the spinner

puts the amount indicated (1, 3, 4 or all) into the pot.
For 'put-all', the spinner doubles the amount in the pot.
If the top falls with a 'take' side uppermost, the spinner
takes the amount indicated. For 'take-all', the spinning
player takes all the money in the pot.

VARIATION: TWISTER

Another spinning game of chance, twister is still played
at The Brickmaker's Arms in Norwich and The
Horseshoes at Alby, Norfolk.

The twister wheel is divided into twelve sections, each
coloured black or red in alternating sequence and each
painted with a number from 1 to 12. The numbers are
random, not in any sequence. In the centre of the wheel
is a spinner which turns freely when nudged.

Players either compete to have the highest spin, after
each player has had a spin, or to be the first to reach
100 points.

In some pubs, the player with the lowest-value spin
buys a round of drinks.

Guessing games

MORA

This is a guessing game for two players using their fingers.

Playing

The two stand, or sit, opposite each other, each with both hands on the chest in closed fists. A third person is needed to give a starting signal. When the signal is given, both players throw their hands forward, shouting at the same time.

The throw

This is to show a chosen number from 0 to 10 using fingers and thumbs. Nought is indicated by both hands being thrown forward as closed fists. For a number of five or less, one hand will be thrown with a closed fist.

The shout

In turn, each player calls out the number he or she guesses the opponent will 'throw'. The players can shout any number from 0 to 9. For a guess of 10, a player shouts 'mora'.

Winning the round

The player who shouts correctly wins the round. If both shout correct guesses, the round is a draw. If neither guess is correct, neither scores a point.

Winning the game

A game of mora can have from ten to fifteen rounds; the number should be agreed before starting. A point can be scored for each round won or drawn. The player with the highest number of points wins the game. If there is still a draw, the game should be played off by a

best of three rounds until a clear winner emerges.
If bets are laid, the winner takes all the money staked
by both players.

How the hands can be thrown

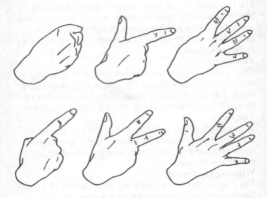

VARIATION: SHOOT
In this variation, players throw their fingers as in mora,
but the shout is either 'odds' or 'evens' to guess
whether the number of fingers will be odd or even.
Nought counts as an even number.
The winner of each round and of the game is
determined as for the game of mora.

SPOOF

Related to up jenkins (p.242), this is an intriguing game
of bluff for at least three players, in which each person
tries to guess the total number of objects the players are
concealing in their hands.

Playing

Each player has three small objects, such as coins or
matches. The players hide any number of their objects
(or none if they wish) in one of their outstretched fists.
One by one, in a clockwise direction, the players call
out the total number of objects they think are contained
in all the players' hands – but no two players may say
the same number.

When all the players have guessed, they open their fists
and the objects are counted. The player who guessed
correctly, or whose guess was nearest to the correct
number, wins the round.

Bluffing

In this game, much depends on the ability to determine
whether a player is bluffing when guessing. For
example, guessing high might indicate that the caller
has a full hand of three objects (especially if he or she
happens to be the first caller in the round). Similarly,
guessing low could mean a low number of objects – or
an attempt to deceive the players as to the contents of
the hand.

Drinking variation

Some rules state that the winning player drops out, and
the remaining players continue for another round, the
winner of which drops out. Play continues until only
one player remains, who then must buy a round of
drinks.

Spoof: possible combinations with three players

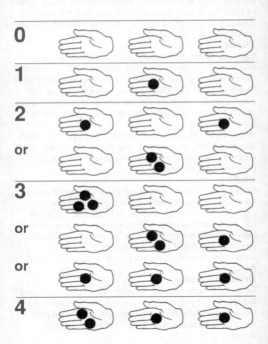

Spoof: possible combinations with three players (cont.)

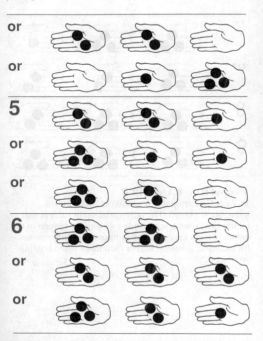

Spoof: possible combinations with three players (cont.)

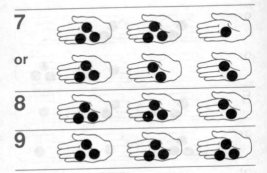

VARIATION: KANNOBLE

In West Country pubs, a version of spoof called kannoble is played. The only variation in rules is that on the final round, when only two players remain in the game, players may not make impossible bluff guesses – for example, guessing higher than three when holding no objects.

UP JENKINS

Known as tippet in the cities of Manchester and
Salford, up jenkins became very popular in pubs all
over Britain during the 1930s. Although the courts had
ruled that all pub games should be locked away on
Sundays, up jenkins and its many local variations could
be played discreetly, with no more equipment than a
small coin, so it became a favourite Sunday pub game.

Playing

A single small object, such as a coin, ring or die, is
used.

One player sits in the middle of a circle formed by other
players. The players in the circle sit with their hands
behind their backs, with one player holding the small
object.

When the player in the middle says 'go!' the players in
the circle all pass, or pretend to pass, the object hand to
hand around the circle behind their backs.

When the player in the middle says 'up jenkins!' the
players in the circle must put their hands palms down
on the ground. The player with the object must, of
course, try to keep the object concealed at this stage of
the game.

The player in the middle then tries to identify which of
the players is hiding the object. If he or she guesses
correctly, the player 'caught' with the object sits in the
middle and becomes the guesser. If the guesser is
incorrect, the passing begins again.

Modern and pay games

Games which can only be played by placing coins in a slot are of two kinds: gambling games and non-gambling games. In either case, the player pays to use the machine.

Both types of games are played using electronic equipment installed either by the brewery that owns the pub or by a games company on contract to the owners.

FRUIT MACHINES

One of the earliest slot machines was the fruit machine. The player won or lost according to how many similar fruit were pictured in line when three or four spinning barrels inside the machine came to rest.

Dozens of variations have been spawned from this simple game. In all cases they are played by one person, who feeds the machine a steady supply of coins in return for the occasional win, carefully designed to keep the punter playing.

The odds, of course, are against the player, although individuals will tell of those rare times when they made a huge win. How much was paid out in order to make the win is never taken into account. In the early days, fruit machines could be relied upon to pay out regularly, and in some pubs and clubs, customers could often accurately assess the moment.

PINBALL

The modern pinball game has been 60 years in the making. During the Depression of the 1930s, pinball games were used in the USA by struggling businesses to attract customers. The end of Prohibition meant pinball could become a bar game, where players drank while they played. Versions were imported to Britain soon after they became popular in the USA.

The '50s was the Golden Age for pinball: the artwork was slick and all essential elements of the modern game were in place, including flippers, slingshot kickers and pop bumpers. In the 1970s and '80s the video invasion threatened to swamp pinball. After a brief period of decline, however, pinball enjoyed a revival.

Although usually found in arcades, where the machines sit alongside video games, today pinball is played in pubs and cafés as well.

The machine

The pinball game is made up of a playing area (tilted down somewhat toward the player), which sits on legs so that it is about waist-high. Behind the playing area and perpendicular to it is the backboard, which advertises the game's theme and holds the area where scores are tallied. Although each pinball game has a different theme and variations of scoring, the basic principle is the same: to shoot steel balls into the playing area and gain points.

Players

Pinball can be played individually or, with many
games, in pairs, one player against the other.

Playing

After inserting the appropriate coin or coins, the player
releases steel balls, one at a time, by pulling on a knob
(plunger) on the front of the machine. The plunger
works on a spring mechanism to shoot the ball into the
playing area. There it bounces against the many
obstacles and bumpers and falls into shallow holes as it
rolls back toward the front of the playing area.

Once a ball returns to the front it is dead, and the player
then releases another using the plunger. The number of
balls per game varies.

The aim of the player is to score as many points as
possible per game by encouraging each ball to hit
obstacles.

Skill

In early pinball games, skill was limited to the initial
plunger shot. Later, the development of flippers added a
new dimension of skill: activated by buttons on both
sides of the machine, flippers allow players to shoot the
ball up toward the back of the playing area, thereby
increasing the chances to score points. The skill lies in
knowing when to activate the flippers.

Another addition was the slingshot kicker, which gives
the ball an extra boost as it bounces off rubber rings,
usually located just above the flippers. Extra-sensitive
bumpers were also added to give balls additional
rebound power.

Tilting

Nudging the machine to manipulate the ball's

movements (called tilting) is not allowed. In 1935 the first electric tilt indicator was invented, which cut off the machine's power if a strong tilt was registered. Such devices are still used on pinball games today.

Bonus scores

Depending on the game, high scorers win bonuses of free games or extra balls.

MUSIC IN PUBS

Although not strictly a pub game, music in pubs has been a long-standing tradition, and many pubs still have a piano and use it for social singing.

The coming of the disco, piped music and electronic versions of the old pianola has turned live music into a special event rather than the norm.

A combination of video with live voices is to be enjoyed on karaoke nights, when brave individuals or whole families can sing with the backing of taped professional pop groups.

Many pubs also hold contests for local entertainers, especially comedy and musical turns.

WORD GAMES

Many games introduced on television find their way into the pubs, where local leagues abound. Quiz games of all kinds have become very popular, and both regular and casual teams can play on quiz nights.

Commercial board games such as the quiz game Trivial Pursuit and television or radio contests, such as BBC's Mastermind, are played in some pubs.

Commercial word games, such as the word-building game of Scrabble, and other board games are often available to play on request.

Record games

The Guinness Book of Records is the source of ideas for record-breaking attempts arranged by many pubs. Some of these are described here.

BARREL ROLLING

Coopers and brewery workers throughout Europe have competed to push full barrels of beer over a measured course.

The pushing is done by a team of men and women. In 1979 the Burton-upon-Trent barrel race took place between teams from many breweries and pubs. The Ind Coope Keg Plant team won it, and the Bass Worthington team were close runners-up.

The record for pushing a 36-gallon (136l) metal barrel of beer over a measured mile was made in 1982 by a team of six men from Nuneaton in Warwickshire.

BUCKET CARRYING

This championship contest seems to have disappeared from Britain. The bucket to be carried was filled with small coins to a weight of 45kg (100lb).

The last contest seems to have been in 1968 when the team of eight from The Balaclava Hotel in Blackburn, Lancashire, beat the team from The Bay and Horses at Beeston Rylands, near Nottingham. Like many similar game-contests, this one may reappear.

CLOG COBBIN'

Flinging footwear seems a popular game in some areas and it is not surprising that – in the counties where clogs were worn to protect the wearer's feet at work – a clog-throwing contest was started by the landlord of

The Hargreaves Arms at Lumb near Bacup, Lancashire, in the 1970s.

A typical clog weighed 1.1kg (2.5lb), being made of thick leather with steel toe caps. Metal studs held the top to the hard wooden soles. Sparks would fly when the wearer walked across cobbled stones on the way to work.

Throwing the clog

The course along which the clog had to be thrown was marked every 3m (10ft) with a brick. The player had to throw the clog between his or her legs, so the moment of release was critical and onlookers had to take care not to be in the firing line.

Scoring

Teams of five from local pubs competed against each other. Players in opposing teams were paired off, each having two throws. The one making the longest throw won the pairs contest. The match was won by the team having made the best five throws.

COAL CARRYING

On Easter Monday, the annual coal-carrying championship starts from The Royal Oak pub at Gawthorpe, near Leeds.

The course is 987m (1080yd) uphill to the village maypole. Male contestants carry a bag of coal weighing 50.8kg (112lb) the full length of the course. Female contestants carry a 12.7kg (28lb) bag of solid fuel over a 91m (100yd) sprint.

PEA-PUSHING

In the 1970s pea-pushing contests were held regularly at the Eclipse Tavern in Tunbridge Wells, Kent. The contestant had to push a (dried) pea up a stretch of cobbled road outside the pub, 12.8m (14yd) long. The difficulty lay in the method of pushing, which was done on hands and knees, using only the nose!

STRAW AND WOOL CARRYING

The Oxenhope Straw race involved teams carrying bales of straw from pub to pub in Yorkshire. In the Tetbury Woolsack race, individuals compete to carry a sack of wool weighing 25kg (55lb) up to the top of the Tetbury hill.

WELLIE WANGING

Throwing the wellington boot is said to have begun in Gerrigong, New South Wales, Australia in 1971. To partake in a modern contest the boot must be a size 8 Challenger made by Dunlop.

The current records for throws by men and women, respectively, are 52m (173ft) and 39.6m (129ft 11in).

YARDS OF ALE

The inns of England have challenged their clients to drinking contests since at least Anglo-Saxon times. The most common drinking game still to be found in many pubs all over the country is yards of ale. In Stratford-upon-Avon there is a pub called The Yard of Ale which has a fine collection of yard-of-ale glasses available for contests on request.

An annual contest is held on Good Friday at The Greyhound pub in Tinsley Green, Sussex, while The Hollybush at Priors Marton in Warwickshire has a contest on April Fool's Day.

The yard-of-ale glass
Traditionally made from hand-blown glass (though some modern yards are made from plastic), the yard-of-ale glass is 91cm (36in) long. It is trumpet-shaped at the drinking end, and at the other end is a spherical bulb.

Depending on the size of the bulb, the yard holds 2.5 to 3 pints of ale.

Not all yard-of-ale glasses are a yard long – they can be as short as 76cm (30in) – nor is there always a bulb, but a straight glass tube does not offer the drinker much of a challenge.

The contest

The original purpose was to test the drinker's manliness, though women now take part and the test is now one of how quickly rather than how much.

Contests are timed, and the winner is the person who drinks the whole yard of ale, without spillage, in the shortest time.

Records

Many records have been made and broken over the years. For example, Peter Edwards drank a 2.5-pint yard in ten seconds at The White Lion in Portway, Worcestershire, in 1957, but Peter Dowdeswell cut the time to five seconds for a 3-pint yard at The Royal Oak, Bishops Cleeve, Gloucestershire, in May 1985.

Techniques

Most beginners end up drenched in ale. The secret is to tip the glass very slowly and sip continuously. A point is reached where there is an airlock in the bulb which forces the ale down the tube more quickly. The final problem to be overcome is at the end when the drinker must tip the bulb high enough to drain it without the ale rushing down to drench the drinker.

COLLINS GEM

Other Gem titles that may interest you include:

Gem Card Games

A handy guide that explains the rules and strategies of play for a wide variety of popular family card games **£3.50**

Gem Card Games 2

A selection of over 80 competitive card games to be played for stakes **£3.50**

Gem Travel Games

An indispensible help in keeping children amused on journeys **£3.50**

Gem Games for One

A compact guide to over 100 games and activities to play by yourself **£3.50**

Gem Family and Party Games

A guide to the rules and methods of play for nearly 300 family and party games **£2.99**

COLLINS GEM

Bestselling Collins Gem titles include:

Gem English Dictionary (£3.50)

Gem Calorie Counter (£2.99)

Gem Thesaurus (£2.99)

Gem French Dictionary (£3.50)

Gem German Dictionary (£3.50)

Gem Basic Facts Mathematics (£2.99)

Gem Birds (£3.50)

Gem Babies' Names (£2.99)

Gem Card Games (£3.50)

Gem World Atlas (£3.50)

All Collins Gems are available from your local bookseller or can be ordered direct from the publishers.

In the UK, contact Mail Order, Dept 2M, HarperCollins Publishers, Westerhill Rd, Bishopbriggs, Glasgow, G64 2QT, listing the titles required and enclosing a cheque or p.o. for the value of the books plus £1.00 for the first title and 25p for each additional title to cover p&p. Access and Visa cardholders can order on 041-772 2281 (24 hr).

In Australia, contact Customer Services, HarperCollins Distribution, Yarrawa Rd, Moss Vale 2577 (tel. [048] 68 0300). **In New Zealand**, contact Customer Services, HarperCollins Publishers, 31 View Rd, Glenfield, Auckland 10 (tel. [09] 444 3740). **In Canada**, contact your local bookshop.

All prices quoted are correct at time of going to press.